Seconds Please

Lesson on life, love and self after divorce

Seconds Please

CARLA DA COSTA

Trade Paperback ISBN: 978-0-6451392-9-7
eBook ISBN: 978-0-6452626-0-5

Print information available on the last page.

The kind press acknowledges Australia's First Nations peoples as the traditional owners and custodians of this country, and we pay our respects to their elders, past and present.

THE
KIND
PRESS

www.thekindpress.com

To the men who graced my life and gifted me the journey
my soul needed to have.
Thank you.

And to me. For never allowing myself to stay stuck or
where I didn't belong, for longer than I needed to be. You've
learnt to have an easeful presence and centredness that you
didn't always have. I am proud of you.

CONTENTS

Preface

This is the book I wish I'd had when I found myself single after being in a relationship and married for thirteen years.

When I left my marriage, I left hoping for a happily-ever-after love story. Instead, I found myself on a personal growth journey. One I never asked for or expected. One I didn't want!

I had expected a straight line taking me from one long-term relationship to my next. Instead, I found myself on something entirely different. A less than straight journey that has taken me to where I needed to be; yes, from point A to B, but in a much different way than I could ever have imagined or anticipated.

I'd love to tell you that my journey has been all sunshine, rainbows and unicorns, but it would be a half truth. One that glosses and skips over so much. The juicy bits, the unlearning, the learnings and the exploring.

I happily share this because I know that this path after leaving a long-term relationship or marriage, after so many years out of the dating pool, is similar for most of us.

In my close circle of friends, I was the first one to separate and get a divorce. Everyone around me was either still happily married or at least pretending to be.

It did feel like somewhat of a failure to be *that* couple.

Our separation came as a shock to most people around us. Outwardly, you could have said that we were the perfect couple. Good looking. Young, with so much ahead of us. Living in an inner-city suburb in a home we owned. Parents to two beautiful daughters. A great social media reel sharing photos of our daily life and travels. A small business we owned together. A beautiful family life.

The white-picket-fence life was real.

Ultimately, so was the façade.

I never saw coming the ripple effect that my separation and divorce would have on those around me. My friendships changed. My close friends who were still married were supportive but couldn't fully understand many of the life changes I was experiencing. My singleness and decision to leave my marriage triggered some of my friends to almost protect their own marriage—because these things are 'catching', you know!

My single-life journey became something they envied in parts, but something they couldn't quite understand or resonate with either.

My mum felt deep fear for me, worried that my post-marriage journey might mirror her own. Her fears projected lovingly but unhelpfully onto me. 'The grass is not always greener, Carla, you might regret this one day.' (Let me tell you, I have not and the grass is definitely greener.)

Getting a divorce felt like throwing all the balls of my life up into the air while I stood below, waiting to see where everything was going to land. Everything I cared about hanging in uncertainty—an emotion I eventually had to get used to moving through life with so I could survive this period.

Our children. Our family. Our finances. Our life together. All pulled apart because I was no longer happy—that word. Because I couldn't pretend any longer. Because I had woken up to the realisation that I had so much more life left to live and that I couldn't keep living it in the way I had been.

There is nothing more uncertain than going through a separation and divorce. It's one of those four Ds alongside death, disaster and debt that changes everything once you walk through it for a reason.

You walk in one person. You walk out another.

It's confronting. It's frightening. It triggers every fear you knew you had and every fear you didn't realise you were carrying. But ultimately, it is so much more than that for your soul. It is liberating. It is empowering. It is so fucking freeing to admit out loud, 'This isn't working and I can't do this anymore.'

The hardest break up to have is the one you don't want to see happen, but know deep down needs to happen so you can both happily live on in your lives.

That was definitely us. And I feel my ex would now agree with me on this too.

Despite everything, I would choose all of this for myself every time, again and again. Over and over.

If I had to live my life over, I'd choose to marry my ex-husband again. I'd choose to divorce him and move on to the next season of my life without him as my partner also. I have learnt so much about myself. Grown so much as a person.

Realised who I really am underneath it all. To have a life that feels as good on the inside as it looks on the outside—once you're in this place—is absolutely everything. The feeling of oneness and relief is something else.

Free to be me. Free to be all of me.

Hindsight and my personal journey have allowed me to see the full breadth of my life: The woman I was, the woman I am and the woman I am now free to be.

Free to have a life that fills me with a deep happiness and passion.

A love that aligns with who I am now and not who I used to be.

The confidence and zeal to be my fullest, most expressed self.

I am an enthusiastic, full-body yes to my 'Seconds Please!' and to this next season of me. I have embraced her fully and continue to do so.

My ninety-year-old self, sitting back in her rocking chair, will look back on this time that I've lived and know she would choose this for herself again every single time. She will see that this was the point in my life where my heart was cracked wide open. This was the moment where everything changed for me. Where I stepped into my own and never looked back.

There is so much brilliance in that.

With love to you xx

PART ONE
Okay, so now you're single

♥

(Whether you asked for it or not)

Congratulations ...

Or is it too early for that? Either way, you've just passed a life-cliff moment, without even realising you have.

No one gets married hoping they will one day get a divorce. The decision to leave a marriage and undo all of its parts—the love, the financials, the children, the family, the expectations of others around us—is a massive one.

The repercussions of leaving a marriage, even when it's an ever-increasing possibility in our minds, can feel enormous. The price, too high. The uncertainty of how life could look in the future after leaving, too much to even begin to process.

Will I end up one of those women all alone for the rest of her life? Will I find love again? Will my children hate me? Will someone love and accept my children as well as me? Will I struggle financially? What will my family and friends think?

It's why many couples can stand at this relationship life cliff for a very long time, weighing up what to do next. And do nothing.

Do I take the leap and leave?

Do I stay and make the best of what we have together?

Some of us here chose to jump. We took the leap and made the decision to leave. We saw the writing on the wall, listened to our feelings and called it.

Some of us here were pushed. It wasn't our choice. We wanted to stay married. Hoped to make things work and saw all the ways and reasons that it could and should.

There is no side better than the other. The only important thing here is to recognise which one you are.

The jumper or the one who was pushed?

Because those who jumped most likely have landed on their feet. They were expecting it, planning for it even, weighing it up long before they leapt—which doesn't make the ending of a marriage any less painful, but the level of acceptance and preparedness is already there.

The dream future they signed up to when they said 'I do' had already begun to dissolve. They are on their feet now, they feel ready even if they're not and they are looking around at the new future that is in front of them. They might be feeling guilty, they might not even be moving forward yet (or maybe they are), but they're definitely thinking about it.

And for those who were pushed … well, most likely you landed flat on your face because you weren't expecting it. You hadn't asked for it. You still had hope. And even though you may have felt it coming, it still feels like a shock. There is a level of needing to dust ourselves off that comes with landing on our face.

You can't avoid it or wish to be in any other place than you are right now. As much as you might try, it can't be ignored. The shock to self, to the dream future and legacy that is no longer can feel soul destroying for this person.

Whether you jumped or were pushed, whether you were one of those rare couples who jumped together, holding hands and supporting each other all the way down, be kind and compassionate to yourself and one another. To your ex-husband also, even if he doesn't really deserve it.

Your journeys may look different. Your movement forward into the next chapters of your lives may be going at different paces and in different directions.

One of you may appear to be doing it with more ease than the other. But your paths, let me tell you, will ultimately be the same in time.

Even if it doesn't look and feel that way now.

You will come eye to eye further down the line.

Trust your path.

One of you will be this person and one of you will be that one

When a relationship ends, I see this pattern occur in almost every instance. Both of you will move on in your own time. However, one of you will stay very much the same person and the other will change, growing and evolving into a completely different version of themselves. Without meaning to.

If we reflect on this, this phenomenon makes sense. Because a healthy, fulfilling relationship ideally consists of two people continually growing and evolving into themselves individually. Choosing to return together in love, alongside one another through it all.

When one of us stops growing, when one of us begins to contract and pull back in emotional, physical or sexual ways, things are almost always starting to brew. And none of it is usually positive.

Stagnancy.

The intimacy dies.

Resentment.

Boredom.

Loss of passion.

Disconnection.

If this dynamic hadn't existed, the marriage would have probably continued into the happily ever after. Two open-hearted, evolving and growing individuals moving and loving one another alongside their life journey.

So what do I know to be true here?

The person who stays very much the same will move on quickly in their new life. Maybe through their life or professional experience, during the marriage they were already living their life path or the one they wish to live. They are already living at their fullest self-expression. The only thing they need is a partner who is a supportive match to their existing desires and life path. They are happily content in their own skin and life, regardless of your feelings or thoughts about it!

Often a woman's self-growth does take a back seat in a relationship because she has had children. This is usually the equation here.

Someone did need to raise and nurture the children. This role often falls to the woman. And someone needed to continue to earn money and strive in their career. This role often falls to the man.

The person who will stay very much the same will most likely go on to choose a new partner for themselves quickly. They will avoid being on their own and choose to jump straight into a new relationship as soon as they can, literally replacing their ex with someone else. Perhaps with someone similar to their ex!

They know what they want and who they are. And they will choose a partner and life that supports them to stay this version of themselves.

They will look like a success post divorce. Moving on

beautifully and kicking goals. Kudos to this person. If you're on a winning formula, you know who you are and you're not hurting anyone, then stick with what's working for you!

Whether this is you or not, know this about this person: The same personal and relationship issues that caused their relationship to break down and end before will follow them into their next relationship if they are not explored and resolved.

Life is a series of lessons and what we choose to not face about ourselves in the present moment only ever presents itself to us later in another moment. The same lesson, just dressed up in different clothes. Ahhh, the universe is brilliant like that!

Until we learn it, the lesson will continue to present itself to us.

I once said to my ex-husband's girlfriend when she made a complaint about him to me: 'I don't know what to say. He's the same guy I met when I was twenty-one, only now he's older, drives a better car and has a bigger house.'

While this might not be entirely true, also it kind of is. I love my ex-husband anyway!

So, if you're not the one staying the same, this makes you the grower out of the two of you.

Hello, kindred, aligned and growing soul. In life, we can only avoid the growth we need to do for so long before the universe makes us so uncomfortable that we can no longer ignore it.

I see you. You're changing life paths. Upgrading your inner hardware. Ascending higher to a life and lifestyle that feels more aligned with who you really are. Levelling up your soul system within.

Who even were you? Did you even know who you were before? Who the hell are you now?

I liken this process of changing life paths and upgrading our inner hardware to finally skipping the scratch on a record we've been stuck going over and over. It's a literal picking up of the needle and placing it forward onto the next song.

We always knew deep down that there was a next song to enjoy. We always felt a silent desire and pull to explore it and move on.

Welcome to your own personal growth journey, where in five years' time you will look back on yourself today and wonder how you were ever married to that guy for as long as you were and how you tolerated it.

Like your own personal game of Jumanji, you are going to start ascending higher through levels of evolving, self-discovery, undoings and reconnecting with self that you need to master. Placing you eventually on the path to discovering and living as your higher self.

You at your absolute best.

This is going to be more than just about finding a new partner for yourself—sorry to tell you this if you thought this was the journey. This is you choosing life and love from your worth and not from your wound.

The call to stay the same is tempting, I won't deny. It's a warm bath of familiarity and comfort. I never judge anyone else's journey or what they choose to do. Neither should you. Each to their own divine journey.

Change is often uncomfortable but the result is ALWAYS stunning and beautiful. Cue image of a butterfly slowly emerging from its cocoon.

If you have unwittingly found yourself on the path of growth and change, embrace it. It's where you need to be and your life will forever be changed by what you embrace and move through in this space of time.

While your ex who stayed the same might outwardly look like a success post divorce, ticking all the boxes relationship-wise, career-wise and financially, you perhaps, for a little while, outwardly might not. Your journey might look a little slower, your wins might look small or non-existent to others. But know that your life will carry you to where you need to be, at the right time for you, and it will be even better than you can imagine now.

It always does.

Trust me.

Women leave in their head first, men with their feet

A woman is often done in her head long before she leaves with her feet. This is almost always true. There's a certain line that a woman crosses in her head of *I'm done*. Once crossed, there's really no calling her back over it.

She's gone.

She might stay for the kids, might stay for financial reasons, but in her head, she's making love to the cute guy at the gym, the guy friend who listens and understands her emotionally, anyone to make her feel like a passionate, appreciated woman again. This was certainly my journey. And if you're the one who chose to leave your marriage, it is probably yours too. I expressed my emotions. Felt unheard and shut down. I closed myself emotionally and then I shut down physically on my marriage. I closed up sexual shop for twelve months and I weighed up my guilt, wondered whether our relationship could actually ever improve for the long term, considered my future if I were to leave and sat with its possible impact before I finally decided to leave.

I won't touch on men here other than to say that biologically they are wired differently and we should never compare ourselves.

In these pages, I want to gift you the freedom and release to know it's not just you feeling and moving through a relationship ending in this way. It is almost everyone. After years of working with women in this season of their life, believe me when I tell you that this is very much true.

Sometimes letting go of the dream is harder than letting go of the actual person

It's not really letting go of the past that is the problem.
It is coming to terms with letting go of a possible future that
will never be. That is the struggle. The mind wants to keep its
fantasies. Even when they are wrong, unhealthy, dangerous,
or even cruel. To let go of the past you must let go of the
future and live in the present.
— The Idealist

I left my marriage of my own choosing, but by no means did I leave it high fiving the world and kicking up my heels with glee. I left my marriage carrying a lot of hurt, disappointment and sadness.

At what it had been and what it could have been.

At this time in my life, newly divorced and acting like I didn't care, underneath I still kind of did. I was carrying a deep sense of loss at the potential I'd seen in our future together and sadness at the now gaping chasm between what I'd always hoped would be my story and what I could now see was the reality.

A marriage ending is a grieving process and, depending on how it ended, you either grieved for its loss while you were married or you will grieve for its loss after it ended. Or like me, both.

Either way, there is a grieving, and often it is always more about the loss of the dream than it is the loss of the actual person.

I didn't realise how much hope I'd had and possibility I'd seen in our relationship until Facebook did that lovely thing it sometimes does and shared a memory with me. It was a photo I'd taken of my then-husband on our honeymoon, and if any photo could capture the hope and love I'd had for our future, this was the photo. Seeing it on my screen that day as I scrolled down my phone, literally sat me down.

It wasn't the loss of him. It was the loss of us and all we could have been into the ends of our years. It was all that potential. Now wasted. Gone.

Grief is a funny thing. It comes and goes in waves, whatever the death might be—a person passing away, a dream ending, the loss feels the same.

Grief is not a straight line. When you think you are over it, life shows you a memory and you realise you are still quite not.

Walking away from a marriage, whether by choice or consequence, moves very much in the same way. Just when you think you're good, your ex will move on or move to another suburb, or your children will go from living at yours most of the time to living at their dad's just as much.

There is always a new something to grieve and adjust to, until one day there is not.

I'm not sure if grief really ever goes away, or if grief one day just turns itself into gratitude and beautiful memories without you realising it has transformed itself. I think it's more we just learn to live without something we once thought we couldn't.

But know, grief always does become easier to live with if we let go and allow it to pass.

Don't sit yourself out, please

I hear many women say they're done with love. A lot of women think and feel this way at different parts of their journey out of love and a marriage. Men do too, of course. It's easy to leave a marriage and to feel jaded about love. I've heard it all.

'I'll never get married again.'

'I'll never live with someone again.'

'I couldn't take being hurt again like this. I'd rather be on my own.'

When I hear these things what I know I'm really hearing is, *I'm hurting*. And what I know is really going on is that they haven't stopped hurting enough to meet the right person for themselves yet. That person who will sweep in out of nowhere and change everything for them, cracking their heart wide open again in the process.

That person who finds love again is actually the majority. The person who chooses to stay on their own, or ends up on their own, forever hiding from love, is the minority.

You might not see this now, but I do. Please don't sit yourself out. You're hurt now. This doesn't mean you will be hurt forever.

Let yourself feel however you do. And know you won't be in this space forever.

You divorced the same person you married. They didn't change ... you did

I have a handful of life moments where truth slapped me in the face and brought me to my knees.

Myself, lying naked on the floor of a beautiful rainfall-style shower at the Alex Hotel, post moving out of our marital home, has to be one of my more profound.

In that moment, all the pain that my past choices had caused me literally had me floored. It continues to be a life moment that brings tears to my eyes when I think about it.

The pain of my own mistakes was simply so overwhelming and deep, it was immobilising. In that moment I'd never felt more abandoned and let down by those around me. And I'd never felt more abandoned by my own self.

I had spent my adult life mostly putting everyone's needs and intentions for me above my own. In a way living someone else's life path. Playing a supportive role in my husband's life with no real thought to my own because he had been the stronger personality with the bigger, more ambitious goals.

Now I was paying the price.

In that shower moment, with the steaming hot water falling down on me, I realised that where I found myself shouldn't be coming as any surprise.

Self-abandonment is a thing. Almost a bigger thing than

when others abandon us. It cut deeply to acknowledge to myself all the times I'd dismissed my intuition and acted against it, ignored and downplayed my feelings, let myself be shut down, bitten my tongue or pretended I didn't need in my life what I did—connection, affection, intimacy, kindness, understanding.

Funny how you can tolerate so many things for the sake of a marriage until one day you just cannot.

I changed the rules on my ex-husband when I asked for a separation and divorce. He was content with how things were. They suited him. He might not have been 'happy' but he was 'ok' and for him that was close enough.

And of course, our marriage was going to feel ok for him. I'd enabled him to be the way he was and to stay that way for as long as he had.

It was me who changed the rules on him. Me who changed their mind. Me who said, 'I'm done.'

So when it came to the week of packing up and moving out of our marital home, rather than the support I had been expecting from my ex-husband—because I saw our marriage failing as a reflection of us both—I received a 'you wanted the divorce, so you can do the packing up' response.

And just like that, he took his new girlfriend away for a holiday (because he was the person choosing to stay the same and already living his life path), and left me with our two daughters, both under the age of four, to pack up an entire house and move out on my own.

Thank God for good friends, who helped me pack the cutlery and all those time-consuming small pieces. Thank

God for good friends, who picked me up off the hotel shower floor. Thank God for the boyfriend who I'd been seeing for six months and who chose to break up with me in the middle of it all.

He too was going through a divorce and couldn't be there for me during my own.

We do always meet our mirrors—including during those times!

There are many beautiful, amazing things that come with being a resilient, strong human being, which I am. We can withstand much of what life throws at us with strength, grace and steadfastness. But it also means that it takes a shit tonne of shit to crack us open and make us face our own pain and shadow, as we all need to at times in our life.

I could have withstood the solo move physically and emotionally. I'm robust like that! I was coping and mostly good … right up until my boyfriend, who I had hoped was going to save me from all of this mess, broke up with me. He was the straw that broke the camel's back in that moment. But I am forever grateful for him behaving like he did and for the complete cracking open that it caused me.

I was a thirty-something woman leaving a marriage that her twenty-one-year-old self had willingly chosen. Pursued, even.

My ex-husband had softened slightly during our twelve years together, but he hadn't changed all that much.

I had.

All the things I'd been keeping silent, I could no longer ignore. All the things I'd pretended weren't important to me,

I could no longer deny. All the things I'd repressed, ignored and glossed over were now just sitting, glaring on the surface of my soul, asking me to acknowledge them.

And my ex-boyfriend … he hadn't changed either. He'd always been too focused on himself and his own pain from the start to ever really be able to support me through mine.

I'd willing chosen both of these men and handed myself over to be loved by them. If I were honest with myself, that meant I'd chosen my own pain and heartache. I was walking away from the same men I'd originally said yes to. They hadn't changed.

As I lay naked on the shower floor, I cursed my twenty-one-year-old self for wanting and needing so much to be chosen by someone else, for needing to be in a relationship because it made her feel validated and enough, and for doing this to the point of abandoning her own self and needs.

And I cursed my divorced self for ever believing a man so wrapped up in his own separation pain could ever possibly change enough to be there for mine. For putting energy into saving him, over putting that same energy into saving and creating myself.

But the lesson I've since learnt is that we should never be down on our younger selves for the decisions and choices they made for us. I do believe everything happens for the right reason, every step leads us to the next wonderful one.

Whether you were twenty-one, twenty-five or thirty-five, you made the best decision you could then with everything that you knew about love and life. All you knew about love, relationships and self-worth had been modelled to you by your parents—rightly or wrongly.

And while maybe you were choosing a relationship more from your wounds than your worth, beautifully, so was your ex-partner.

Two souls, moving through life and trying to do their best. How can you be angry with yourself for that? How can you be angry with them for that either?

What a divine and loving lesson of forgiveness of self and others to reflect on. To realise and acknowledge, with the passage of time, how much more you know and see now. And whether your ex is able to share the same perception or not, no matter.

It can still be yours.

Maybe this is why you chose him to be your children's daddy

If you married in your twenties or thirties, something maybe shaped your choice of partner more than you realised at the time.

The draw and desire to procreate is innately built into all of us as humans. It's how we have survived and thrived as a species for as long as we have. It exists within us as a driving desire, without our conscious awareness.

It is primal.

It's why we see constant pairing offs and attend so many weddings in our twenties and thirties. Everyone is not just coincidentally falling in love all at the same time. We are in our best baby-making years! Our bodies, our psyches are driving us to procreate. Marriage is simply the cultural step most of us feel we need to take before we become parents.

Many of us move through this time in our life not realising our bodies are biologically primed and seeking to make babies.

This is especially true for women with our innate, ticking fertility clocks.

So, what am I suggesting here?

That maybe, just maybe, your choice of husband and father of your children was driven more by your primal drive to mix your genes with what you considered to be the best and strongest, most alluring genes you could attract in the pack.

Maybe you were not choosing the best life partner for you, just the best one to procreate with. This perhaps means that your choice of man to marry was more determined by his looks, physical strength, physique, social standing and popularity, and ability to provide you and your future children with financial security and stability than it was by his ability to provide you with long-term fulfilment, laughter and emotional connection.

There's a light-bulb thought!

I want you to pat yourself on the back right now if this rings true to you.

If you had babies with this man, your choice to do so was actually a successful and smart human one for that time in your life. And now you have beautiful children to show for it.

On a primal level, you have actually been a success.

Your choice of gene pool to make babies with was an excellent one—ponder on that one for a moment. Perhaps he wasn't the most ideal of husbands to you, even the best of fathers to your children, but look at the beautiful babies the two of you made together.

Bless.

I chose good stock to mix my genes with. My ex-husband was attractive, popular, athletic, an achiever, security driven. Honestly, from an innate desire and primal drive to procreate, my subconscious chose someone who ticked some big boxes.

In my opinion, he chose pretty well for himself too!

He might have been lacking in some areas of emotional

intelligence, and so was I at that time, but I can see why we both pursued one another. The gene pool was a strong match for one another on both sides.

Our desire to pair up and make babies during our peak fertility window is the strongest human desire during this period of time. It's why so many girls and women choose and chase the popular and attractive ones. They stand out as the best in the pack.

There's a certain level of validation that comes with being chosen by someone who we consider to be desirable and a good match. And there's also that huge pull to combine our genes with the best that we can attract.

What does this mean for you today, particularly if you've moved past the season of wanting more babies in your future?

Understanding.

When your primal urge to procreate was at its peak, you chose amazingly well for yourself and your future offspring. Smart human move by you! This means your relationship is not a failure, nor is its ending.

Not at all.

Biologically, you have spawned a next generation of fit, strong and attractive offspring who will continue your legacy after you have gone.

So, in the game of playing human, you have played the game beautifully well. You have procreated. And as a bonus, you now have time up your sleeve to do other things in life beyond procreating for yourself which brings with it a degree of awareness.

The gift to see yourself and your ex for what you were—

two human beings moving through life with a primal desire to procreate with the best mate we could find for ourselves.

My belief is that after divorce what we now find ourselves seeking something that was not the primary driver during our peak fertility years. We now enter this next season seeking fulfilment and compatibility on a different level. Shared values, similar energy levels, outlooks on life, deep connection, a sense of fun and emotional intimacy are now the important boxes to tick with someone.

Yes, many of us leave a long-term relationship or marriage with a desire to first enjoy freedom. But ultimately, the above is what will make a man or woman 'stop' for their next significant someone. We can find sex and attention almost anywhere if we wished but fulfilment is rare, and even a person not looking for love or seeking a relationship feels that.

Extend full kindness towards yourself if you now understand more about why you chose your partner and stayed for as long as you did. Particularly if you had been viewing your relationship ending as a failure of yours in some way. Whether you had children or not with this man, it's actually not a failure at all.

It was a success on a primal level.

Love the second time around after babies and why it may take longer to find

Procreate and ensure your beautiful genes live on into the future … tick that beautiful big life box off the list.

Now we move on, looking to find in another something a little more elusive—soul recognition that brings with it emotional depth, passion and fulfilment.

That happiness thing. Not too much to ask for at all.

Here's my order, Universe. In your own time, of course, but don't take too long with it!

It can feel like an almost impossible task to even start thinking about putting a request out into the world for such a thing. I mean … are those people and couples even out there?

This is where I am going to agree with you. A little, anyway.

When we take procreation of the table, we are left desiring something we have rarely seen modelled to us by our parents, friends or peers. A mutual love and connection that runs deeper than a desire to stick it out for the sake of children or keep the asset pool together (so romantic!).

Previous generations of parents stuck out unhappy marriages for the sake of children or to keep finances. Current generations, I'm finding, are trying to keep it together and make things work so their children and family enjoy a better experience and legacy than the one they grew up with—even if it's just on paper or more of a façade.

Those who are divorcing today are opting out of both belief systems.

I was lucky to grow up knowing and seeing one of those unicorn couples. My grandparents on my mother's side were all that and more. Certainly not a perfect couple, but their connection ran deep and time ran it deeper.

'Just come in here and talk to me, Marg,' were my grandfather's favourite words. They were sexually fulfilled and intimate to the end, and we used to joke that Nanna had more action than us. They had a shared sense of humour and outlook on life. They saw, loved and treasured all the sides of each other.

I am truly blessed to have watched them in their love. Not everyone gets to witness soul-mate love in real life and know that it does exist.

There is an immeasurable number of men and women to admire and desire pursuing during our best baby making years. Attractive people are everywhere.

And it's why the nice ones so often get left behind during those procreating years in our twenties and thirties. Why the nice ones didn't really catch your eye back then and were so easily friend zoned.

Seeking to find fulfilment and shared values from a relationship is a much different dating game than the one we played to procreate.

As women, the procreation game in our twenties and thirties looked like: be at my physical best, dress to get and keep their attention, be desirable, show up in a way that leaves him wanting more and thinking after me, do what I need to do to ensure the relationship continues moving forward—compromise, turn a blind eye, bite my tongue sometimes and so on.

In this game, the push/pull and chase was part of building attraction.

But the fulfilment game, the soul-recognition game, is much different. Now, what's on the inside is as important as what's on the outside—maybe even more so. Now, how someone makes you feel is as important as how they feel. (Don't bring me your push/pull and chase games here.) And this new dynamic can be much harder to find because you either have that energy with someone or you don't.

The self-work you have done and will do will help your chances of speeding up this search. Fate will play its hand—life's most brilliant, magic essence of what's meant to be coming together of its own accord. And timing is a real thing.

Your journey might have a lot of close-but-not-quite loves. Or it might not. You might be one of those ones who fall with ease into the arms of their next someone.

Or it might be seconds, thirds, or fourths, please for you.

Whichever one, know that there is nothing wrong with you, or necessarily wrong with what you are doing.

Who knows … the guy for you might still be married and deciding what to do—which doesn't mean he's not on the way, just that he's not here yet.

Do you want to be saved or do you want to be fulfilled?

So how are we going to spend this time now between partners and our next life paths?

I was the girl looking to be saved when I first left my marriage. I didn't see it at the time but I do now.

> *Dear future man,*
> *Save me from not feeling good enough because I'm on my own.*
> *Save me from having to find myself.*
> *Save me from learning how to stand on my own two financially independent feet as a woman.*
> *Save me from having to make hard decisions on my own.*
> *Save me from my aloneness.*
> *Save me from having to work on myself.*
> *Save me, please.*

Three weeks after my ex-husband moved out of our family home, leaving me to live in it while we prepared to sell, I locked eyes with a handsome guy on the dance floor of a pub. He caught my attention straight away.

I was newly out of what felt like a loveless marriage, and I can see now that the reason I became attached to this handsome guy so fast was because he made me feel sexy, appreciated and seen after feeling numb for so long. It was enticing after feeling nothing for so long.

I wanted it to be love, and in all honesty I just assumed he was going to be my next long-term relationship and forever guy. I was so well conditioned to be in a long-term relationship that it never crossed my mind it would be a short-term one. Or that maybe all I needed was for it to be a short-term one.

This didn't end so well for me.

People who avoid saving themselves and look for someone else to save them (like I was), often attract and pursue one of two types of people into their life.

Because women are empathetic, nurturing souls, we easily attract men into our lives who need saving too. They become the project to work on instead of ourselves. A project that beautifully distracts us from our own self-work.

Or we attract someone who swoops in, saves us and solves all of our problems! Reads like perfection, but ultimately, we have given our power over from the start in this relationship dynamic. We look to him for our answers and our life path, we give him that role, and ultimately, he will thrive on it. Sometimes to the point of controlling.

My time spent lying face up, naked on the shower floor of the Alex Hotel was when I realised I'd looked to every man in my past to save me in some way. I'd given the keys to my life and self-worth over to my husband as a twenty-one-year-old, only to find my thirty-something self feeling suffocated, stifled and controlled by it all.

And I'd fallen into the arms of my newest boyfriend hoping

he'd save me from myself and my situation. Only to discover he needed saving himself.

Stuff you both.

I'd love to tell you that I sat up from the shower floor in a space of newly found enlightenment after being dumped.

I did not.

I sat up in complete, utter pain.

And I continued needing to be saved. Sometimes seeking out others to save me within the space of a relationship. Other times, I muddied through the self-work on my own.

Until one day, I did not. I was saving myself. In fact, I had saved myself. And now I was looking for someone who'd saved themselves too.

A person who needs saving and avoids saving themselves generally goes on to inadvertently do one of two things to us in a relationship.

Thanks to your love and support, they grow their own wings and fly away on you. You've saved them, healed them and they don't need your saving energy anymore.

Or they will continue to always need you to save them.

I've played both of those roles in love and life. And neither felt good.

I don't recommend them.

Which leads me to my next point.

You are going to learn on people and people are going to learn on you

You are going to hurt people as you move through this period of your life, unintentionally or not. And people are going to hurt you as they move through this period of their life, unintentionally or not.

Sorry to inform you of this. This unavoidability.

This is life, not just after divorce. This is life at any time.

Humans will always learn more about themselves through their relationships with others than they ever will learn on their own.

Let's be honest with ourselves here. It's easy to perceive ourselves as having our shit together when there's no one reflecting back to us that we do not.

The wiser and more attentive we are, realising that everyone is learning on one another, the better, more compassionate human beings we are. And this is true in life and relationships in general.

This doesn't mean there will be a cascade of heartbreak coming for you in your future—just that this is how humans move through life, in both their energy of kindness and of malice. There are more good people in the world than there are bad. There are more well-intentioned people than there are narcissistic and self-serving. Always remember that.

Every human is simply moving through life, seeking to have their needs met in some way. Their needs for love, for connection, financial security and success. For fun, for fresh air, for significance, for purpose. When we start taking more of a living-above-the-Matrix view on life, over being caught in the middle of it, you will observe men, women and children doing just this.

I need to feel loved—how can I feel this in this moment?

I need to feel peace—how can I create this?

I need to feel fit and alive in my body—what will I do today to feel more like this?

We learn and unlearn on others throughout our entire life. It's best to look at most adults as human beings who were hardwired as children to move through life, trying to get their needs met in the best way possible.

Mum and Dad showed us what love looked like and how to behave so we could continue to receive love from them. And as adults, we seek out and recreate the same energy and feel of what we were modelled. Or in some instances, where our childhood was somewhat negative, we deliberately choose something different for ourselves.

Any relationship that we choose early on in life is most likely going to be based on our childhood conditioning. One chosen much less from a point of adult awareness—which makes sense, because in our twenties and thirties we are in many ways still growing into adults.

What does this mean? We chose someone to marry not really understanding why we chose them.

They made us feel good. They chose us, which made us

feel good enough. Desired what we desired. Moved in the same or similar social circles. They came from a similar socioeconomic background or better. It made sense. Looked and felt sensible and it was more than likely met by approval from your family and friends.

But none of this takes into account what's really going on underneath. The relating styles that both bring to the relationship. The attachment styles we arrived with that we learnt from our parents. The unrealised traumas and the beliefs—both positive and negative—that exist due to our upbringing.

We all carry these patterns and dynamics, whether we are aware of it or not, into our first marriage, and as a consequence this relationship often bears the brunt of much of them being played out in a cycle.

I brought my parents' behaviours, expectations and fears into my first marriage despite them being amazing parents. And my ex-husband brought his.

When I look back at the undoings of our marriage—our dynamic as a couple as we bounced off one another during our thirteen years, everything that we brought out in one another without meaning to, the good and the bad—none of it now comes as a surprise.

We are not to blame for this phenomenon.

This is life.

Some couples genuinely move through their own unlearnings together and emerge a better, more connected couple for doing so.

The love grows, the intimacy deepens. But for many

couples. Their relationship left carrying the cost and burden of unlearning accidentally on each other with other dynamics— resentment, loss of trust, lack of sex or sex being used as a tool to manipulate, emotional shutdowns, a lack of honesty, words being left unsaid and financial manipulation.

I used to envy the couples in their late forties and early fifties after my divorce. Their families, their deep history, finances and everything they built as a couple still together.

But now, I don't. After years of working with many people who feel stuck in these relationships, I see too many falsities and self-compromises in so many of them. It's not because I don't believe in marriage or long-term relationships. It's not because I don't believe they're possible. I deeply do. Only now I believe in only being in the right one. In relationships that genuinely light up my inner and outer world.

Most of us will move through a number of wound-mate-style relationships before we evolve into a space where we are open and ready for more of a deeper connected love.

I've learnt that the most poignant question in our journey into our next love is *How soul-mate ready am I really?*

Ready enough that I am able to consciously stop cycling myself through versions of the same wound-mate relationship—different guy, treating me in a similar/the same way, with the same result. Consciously choosing to not go there.

Because what I do know is this: We will continue to attract a similar shade of the same person until we've done the loving work on ourselves.

Truth.

Soul mates and wound mates (which one were you?)

Soul mates are rare, but it's not because they don't exist.

It's because we as humans are only just beginning to feel culturally 'able' to release relationships and marriages that no longer serve us. An undoing process that ultimately opens us up to entering our next level of partnership, evolving with us as we evolve upwards in ourselves.

Can you see the beauty in this? This ability to ascend higher in love by detaching from the idea that it must be our first love who must be the person for us.

Can you see that the only thing stopping it from unfolding beautifully of its own accord, that keeps us stuck in our wound cycle, is our perception and fear of how long the process might take to find that love. Fears that we might end up alone, unloved or financially struggling? (Whichever fear it might be for you.)

Many of us, in our early adulthood, chose a wound-mate-style relationship first or even several times over for ourselves without realising. Often cycling through many wound-mate relationships, encountering shades of the same people and results, until we eventually (hopefully!) evolved ourselves forward.

So, which one were you—wound mates, or soul mates?

Wound mates

- Relationship feels like it's on a cycle of drama and the same issues repeat themselves and never fully resolve.
- Connection based on unresolved trauma, low self-worth, low self-belief. The relationship validates your need to look and feel good enough.
- You seek to fix or save each other.
- Feels intoxicating, chaotic, addictive and unpredictable. Push/pull energy.
- Reflects unhealthy dynamics with parents and childhood experience.

Soul mates

- Relationship feels healing. You feel seen, heard and appreciated for being you.
- Shared values, outlook on life, vitality. The connection supports you growing together as individuals and as a couple.
- You empower each other.
- Feels grounded and consistent, and flows.
- Relationship has been consciously created and comes together as a result of each individual's growth. The relationship is not a reflection of your parents' dynamic nor a deliberate attempt to be in something different from your parents' dynamic. It just is.

I know that in my own life, I was not an energetic match for a soul-mate relationship in my twenties. I wouldn't have attracted one nor pursued one. I was not ready for such a love. The flow and calm would not have felt attractive or push/pull enough. And I couldn't have possibly held such a thing because I didn't have the emotional awareness.

I would have wasted such a love.

I was not ready for it.

I had not evolved in myself enough.

My journey is true for many.

Learning on others and others learning on us is our collective spirit evolving at our own loving, upward pace toward a relationship that is closer to that of a soul mate.

Can you see how different this journey is going to be for everyone in its pace and in its lessons?

Depending on our conditioning and past experience, some of us have a little to learn and some of us have a lot.

And that's ok.

What to do if you were in a wound-mate-style relationship and don't want to find yourself in another one

I want you to know how many people are in a space of recovering after leaving a wound-mate-style relationship.

So many.

I want you to know how many people are stuck in wound-mate-style relationships and fear leaving.

So many.

By definition, a soul-mate relationship is this: Two souls coming together who have done or are doing the inner work on themselves.

Neither is a perfectly evolved version of themselves (no one is that), but they have evolved out of their desire and need to be saved, to be living in a cycle of trauma, drama and arguing about the same things. And they are no longer addicted to the energetic push/pull nature that wounded relationships bring.

Instead, someone who seeks or is ready to be in a soul-mate relationship desires flow, calmness, intimacy, affection and shared growth, and is comfortable with being fully seen. The connection is everything to this person. They don't need to be saved and they don't want to save anyone either. They come together with one another and they just are.

I've recently felt this, lived this and seen this in my personal life and I'm not going to lie, putting words on this feeling is hard. But when you know … you know. The difference between a wounded relationship and a soul-mate relationship is in the foundation that you bring to one another.

Energy doesn't lie, here.

So, if we consider what it is that makes a soul-mate relationship—two individuals doing the inner work on themselves—then our role in the journey becomes this: to be a soul who is doing the inner work on themselves.

How can we expect from another what we are not truly doing ourselves? The universe won't deliver on that, #trustme.

A soul-mate-ready man will find you attractive because of your evolved nature too. He is not going to seek out a relationship with a woman who still hasn't found at her core her own stability and sense of self—who is still needing to be saved. Who still seeks constant validation because of her anxiety, wounds and trust issues.

No one seeks perfection. No one is fully evolved. But if you seek the peace, love and commitment of a soul-mate relationship, we first need to be an energetic match for one. We need to evolve into a woman who can hold such a love without fear of it being too good to be true or of it leaving her.

Whether someone is ready or wants to do the work on themselves is their journey. We can only ever control ours. And ultimately, if someone chooses not to do the work on themselves, in my eyes, this is evidence that the relationship is a wound-mate relationship, not a soul-mate relationship— regardless of its potential.

Do the work on yourself, beautiful; stay firmly on your life path and move forward with that energy. The right people for you will find you on your journey too. Seek ease, fun and growth, whether or not those around you seek it for themselves.

It's yours to have.

Yes, some people will fall away in the journey, but they are always, ALWAYS, replaced by others more aligned with our truth once we're standing in it.

My marriage ended but theirs didn't ...

Once seen, we can't unsee this wound-mate knowledge. It will change your perception of relationships in your life forever. The ones you have had, the ones you are in and the ones around you.

At least, it did for me.

You will spot the wound mates around you now, doing their best because they genuinely want the best for themselves and for their families. Some will be functioning better than others, or at least presenting the façade that they are.

Healers will tell you that the more soul mates that come together in this world, the higher the level of consciousness it will bring collectively to those around us. An energetic shift from woundedness to love on a collective, generational scale. How divine.

The most beautiful example here is to ask ourselves and imagine, *Who would I be as an adult if my parents had been soul-mate lovers? How different would my choices in love have been?* And if we were to take it another generation onwards: *If I were that person and love had been demonstrated to me in that way as the standard I should expect for myself, then who would that make my children today, having watched me love in that energy?*

People accept, tolerate, excuse and turn a blind eye to many behaviours in the name of love. Or at least to stay in a relationship over not being in one. (Please note in no way am I including situations of domestic violence or fear for personal safety in this statement.)

The truth is that not everyone desires a soul mate. They just want a mate over not having one.

This is going to be why some of your friends and family who are in wound-mate-style relationships will potentially struggle to understand your choice to leave your marriage.

They might have opinions. And they'll either vicariously live through you, watching to see how you go as a measure of how they might if they were to leave their marriage. Or they'll project onto you their own fears and beliefs, my favourites being, 'I'd hate to be out there dating now,' and 'The grass isn't always greener.' Ultimately, these are all their beliefs and fears. Beliefs and fears that are holding them back from moving forward in their own lives. They don't have to be yours.

A lot of people in your life are going to stay in their wound-mate relationships. They will adjust their expectations and behaviour to live with and manage their situation. The truth for us, though, is once we've said goodbye to that wounded cycle, it's very hard to go back into one with our eyes closed.

In all my years coaching clients, I've never had someone leave a wound-mate relationship and look back on it with regret for having left. Their only regret, if they do have one, is that they didn't leave sooner.

Most of our relationships are meant to teach us lessons, not to actually last forever. Not every love is supposed to last.

Feel the freedom over the fear in this.

The truth is, we accept relationships that mirror how we feel about ourselves and we let go of relationships when our soul and spirit can no longer stay quiet and acknowledge we deserve and desire more.

And that journey, that line in concrete of *I deserve more and I can't go back*, is going to look different for everyone.

Oh, the places you'll go

So, where to next?

You're divorced or you're going through the process, which means many of those undoings that cause so much stress have happened or are happening around you.

When I found myself in this part of my divorce journey, I once expected myself to burst out of the gates once it was all finalised. Full of enthusiasm. Full of excitement and no longer feeling weighed down. This was only partly true.

I had the 'I got a divorce party' with my girlfriends. Drank way too much frosé (which was a terrible idea put forth by my friend Dorothy) and celebrated like the occasion deserved. But then life just kind of returned to its everyday cycle.

We all went back to our day jobs, our kids and our to-do lists. And I just sat with my divorce. Excited, yes. Free, yes. Relieved, yes. But what I was to do with it … not really sure.

Just get on with life now, I guess?

There's a phenomenon that occurs when we all of a sudden find ourselves 'free' but don't know quite what to do with that freedom. Almost feel lost with it. We tick the logical, primal needs off the to-do list—find new shelter and safety, find income that supports us, but then what?

Have you heard of the elephant and the rope story?

As a man was passing the elephants, he suddenly stopped, confused by the fact that these huge creatures were being held by only a small rope tied to their front leg. No chains. No cages. It was obvious the elephants could at any time break away from their bonds, but for some reason, they did not.

The man saw a trainer nearby and asked why the animals just stood there and made no attempt to get away. 'Well,' the trainer said, 'when they are very young and much smaller, we use the same-sized rope to tie them and at that age, it's enough to hold them. As they grow up, they are left believing they cannot break away. They believe the rope can still hold them, so they never try to break free.'

The man was amazed. These animals could at any time break free from their bonds but because they believed they couldn't and couldn't see that they could, they stayed right where they were.

Why am I sharing this story with you?

Because when we first find ourselves out of a long-term relationship, so many of us are just like the elephant in the story and are not able to see and embrace all of the freedoms, options and choices that are now ahead of us. All of it can seem too much for someone who previously felt like they had no chance or choice.

Life does not have to look and feel the same for you anymore. The future can look so incredibly different from the past you've just left.

There is so much possible in front of you now.

And you are only limited for as long as you stay tied to the small rope that exists in your mind.

Freedom of choice is exciting, but it can also feel terrifying and paralysing if it's something you've never had full ownership of before, which was my journey. I had not had full ownership over my life and my path ahead ever. I had always lived someone else's life set out for me.

It took me years to completely feel ready to break free of that small rope that held me emotionally in the same place and to start truly venturing forwards, creating my own entirely new world, not one that was an extension of my old one.

I had spent so many years in my marriage feeling like I was in the passenger seat and playing a supporting role to someone else's life—my husband's. We were living his dreams, achieving his goals and discussing his thoughts on what was best to do next.

He was without a doubt, the more driven one and I was the more passive. I lived to help him fulfill his life path.

Now, all of a sudden, I found myself in the driver's seat of my own car. Something I had asked for and wanted, yes, but something I also had no clue what to do with.

I definitely started my journey driving off into the sunset at five kilometres an hour with a wine in hand and a new wardrobe of clothes to look hot in.

Looking the part but not really doing much with it.

I'm proud of that time though. I had a blast!

I did all the cliché things and they worked. The health and wellness retreat on a Fijian island. The reiki. The life coach (it's how I eventually became one here for you). The nude yoga class. You name it, I've tried it.

All of it gently nudged me to see the brilliant, wide-open path in front of me. The path of me now doing whatever I pleased with my life and with my beautiful daughters in tow. And to walk it with courage. Not looking for or needing someone else to walk it with me straight away.

This is all I want you to see in this moment. You having taken your foot out of the rope, just like the elephant could, looking ahead to where you could go and will.

Brilliant.

PART TWO
So where to now?

First, let me tell you where you're really going ...

Sometimes there's what we think we need and want, and then there's what we actually need and want.

Just for a little moment, I'd love for you to remove from the table any desire for love and a new man to come along and sweep you off your feet.

At least while you're reading this chapter!

If you left a relationship that felt loveless for a long time, then I completely understand your desire to find this—love, passion and attention.

If sex, intimacy and connection is something you haven't felt in a long time, then this might be something you need to experience again however it looks or feels. Whether it's 'forever' for you or not. It doesn't matter. And that's called being human. But I also would love for you to consider what this season of your life is really going to be about for you. What it needs to be about for you when you're ready.

You.

So often we hand over our sense of self and trade in our identity as a woman when we marry and become Mum. We don't mean to. It comes with the wife and Mum territory. To identify with both means we were invested in those areas of our life, which is beautiful.

But it's also why women so easily can lose themselves.

I loved being a wife and a mother. Enjoyed sharing and setting up a home for us all. And I loved being a stay-at-home mum. I was so blessed that I was able to be that for the first years of my daughters' lives before they started school. You never get that time back as a mum.

I did all the things. Made Pinterest boards of home interiors and design. Tried out new recipes. Home cooked for my daughters as much as possible and tried to create an environment that was healthy, supportive and loving for them. iPad time, but not too much. Park and beach hangs with friends and their kids. Babycino dates.

All the things.

I really threw myself into the role of Mum and it was a wonderful, blissed-up time in my life.

Then I became the soccer mum and the Uber mum. My time started to facilitate my kid's lives more than it did my own in many ways! But I did it happily, knowing I was creating for them a beautiful, big life of friendships, interests and self-confidence.

The price of this, though, is that we can lose our sense of ourselves as women, separate from being a wife, a mother and everything else to everyone else. Everything becomes about others first.

Women are so easily self-less in this season of life. Men can be too.

Going through a separation and divorce truly moves you into a new season of being a woman, whether you wish to be here or not.

I believe women move through many seasons as we move through life. More than men do. Seasons that often completely change us to our core.

Wife. Mother. Lover. Career woman. Perimenopause. Menopause. All-knowing goddess queen. Grandmother.

I love my daughters with all of my heart. I held on to having them for the majority of time after I left my marriage, for as long as my ex-husband and growing career allowed. They have always been my priority and continue to be.

Now I find myself in a new season. Loving my time with my daughters, of course, but delightfully wrapped up in and enjoying my independence. Rediscovering me for the first real time since I was last single at twenty-one.

And this is the point I'm leading you to … rediscovering you.

One of the biggest positives after a divorce (once you've emotionally adjusted to it) is the time you now have set aside for yourself that is child-free. Time that is now all yours, to do with as you please.

In my marriage, I was the primary caregiver for our daughters. Getting time out and away from them took forward planning and negotiation! It felt like hard work to organise. So for me, it rarely happened.

But now, post-divorce, every second week is delightfully my own.

At first, I felt lost in all this free time away from my daughters. I didn't know what to do with myself, and I had very little to fill this time with, to be honest!

It took time to create, but now that every second week is

wonderfully full to the brim with my life. What I love, who I love, what lights me up, what fills my cup. This week to myself is now all about me and exploring my needs, my desires and my fun. I am very protective of her!

In hindsight, I don't believe women should lose themselves in their children to the point of self-sacrifice. I don't believe it's healthy. I write this fully acknowledging that this is how I moved through that particular season of my life and that I have very few regrets about it.

But still, there is no gold star or prize for taking on that kind of role, only a loss of self that goes on to impact us and impact our relationships.

Rediscovering who you are now as a woman is your journey. Not finding a man who is going to make it all shiny, happy and better.

Sorry!

I know that I didn't want to hear this when I was newly out of my divorce. I wanted the exact opposite. To walk straight into the loving arms of my next someone.

And it did happen like that, as you know. But it didn't end well. As tends to happen.

What you value in a man and what sort of man you need in your life—all of it is going to look and feel different for you now in this season because you are a different woman.

Your journey and life will become yours as much as your children's will become theirs. The more you own yours, the more they will own theirs. I've watched my daughters blossom and grow through the osmosis of watching me as I have blossomed and grown. Every next step up that I take, they take it with me through observance.

Now this is the new normal. Now this is the standard. This is how love looks, sounds and feels for Mum, which is how it will look, sound and feel for me. This is how it looks, sounds and feels for a woman who is stepping into her fullest self-expression and fun, which is how life will look, sound and feel for me.

Can you see how it goes?

Stop living life through your children, if up until now you have been. Stop hiding behind them instead of rediscovering you. Start living life for you again.

This doesn't make you selfish. This doesn't make you less of a mother. This makes you beautifully whole.

Life after divorce is going to be less about finding love for you. It's going to be more about rediscovering you.

The bridge of space and time between relationships

How you choose to spend time between relationships is going to define your next relationship. It will shape who you attract and who you choose to pursue and let in next.

I see so many men and women doing one of two things.

They jump back into the dating pool over and over again—the same person with the same fears of intimacy, the same fears of being fully seen for all shades of themselves, the same feelings of 'I'm not good enough,' the same desire to not be alone, to feel validated. Hoping for a different result.

This is like having the ingredients for a chocolate cake and hoping it's going to come out of the oven an apple cake because you stirred the batter anticlockwise this time instead of clockwise. The same ingredients will always give you the same results. Every time!

Or I see women sitting out of the dating world almost entirely. They just don't have the heart or confidence to put themselves out there again and risk being hurt or disappointed, perhaps occasionally opening their online dating account to see what's out there on a lonely Friday night at home.

Healing between relationships doesn't require a timeline of 'you must be single for this long' or 'you must do this and that'.

Healing does require healing work, though. Time being single without doing some healing work to bring yourself closer to rediscovering you, the woman you are underneath all the layers of guardedness and hurt, is a little bit like lost time. It's hiding, not healing.

And that's ok. But it won't bring you closer into alignment with yourself again so that you can understand why you attract and pursue what you do in love and life and change it. Why you've accepted and settled for breadcrumbs instead of owning your desire to have the whole cake and then some.

The healing is what's going to elevate you to the next level of attracting all that's amazing for you into your life. What you deserve.

Not the tighter booty, not the fancy handbag, not the perfect nails, hair, wardrobe, house or bank account.

None of that truly matters as much as we think it does.

Are you someone who has never really spent time on your own without someone in your bed or in your head?

Welcome to much of the dating pool, if you've dared to venture out there yet! Souls at varying stages, jumping from one relationship and person into the next. All in an attempt to avoid themselves.

Are you excited yet?

Men and women throwing themselves back into the dating pool for the first time in years. Entirely different people to who they were when they were last single, with new wounds and fears—much of it still perhaps unrealised, hoping for a happy result, whether that be short or long term.

It's heartbreaking, in a way, to think about it like this. Grown adults, many of them fearful of being on their own, of ending up alone, seeking to be loved by another to fill the void that being on their own leaves them feeling.

It's no wonder the modern dating pool can sometimes feel like a minefield.

Emotionally avoidant and unavailable people who aren't in a place to be fully invested jump straight into online dating unhealed after a break up. Perpetuating their avoidant cycle by never getting too close or intimate with someone. You can't get hurt again if you only ever keep your connections surface level, right?

And anxious attachers who need and seek out the validation of someone else to feel good enough and loved fall into the trap of these emotionally avoidant love bombers who eventually pull away and trigger their hurt all over again. Perpetuating their own anxious cycle and solidifying their belief that they are not good enough, attractive enough or loveable enough.

In my own dating life, I reached a point where I timed myself out.

And it's not because I'd had a raft of bad experiences or relationships. It's because I could see what I was attracting on repeat, and the dating washing machine I was putting myself in that wasn't giving me the relationship I hoped for.

And in timing myself out, I saw something profound in my journey that I'd never realised or acknowledged before. I was a thirty-seven-year-old woman who hadn't been single or pursued her own thing without the distraction of a man's presence in her life or in her head since she was seventeen.

I'd always had someone.

This is huge for a woman to realise and has more impact on us than it does on men in the same position for several reasons.

In all of my long-term relationships, the man had been the stronger personality and the driver of our relationship. I had played second fiddle to them in many ways. I might have ruled the home, but outside of that, he was more the decision maker, even in those joint couple decisions. I had very much followed his lead.

This is a masculine and feminine balance that exists in all

relationships. Someone needs to take on each of these roles or share them. In a connected, loving relationship, this dynamic is actually beautiful. The masculine is the loving container that holds, leads, supports and cares for the feminine, which allows the feminine to bring the love, fun, spark and grace within the container and to the relationship.

But my dynamic meant that I hadn't had sovereignty over my own life and choices for almost twenty years. For twenty years I lived someone else's life set out for me. And here I was, finally free but feeling out of my own depth and a little lost to find myself on my own for the first time in a long time.

It was deeply triggering. As much as I knew it was where I needed to be, I found the time difficult to enjoy. Found it hard to enjoy the peace in the situation as much as I knew it was good for me.

There is a primal need for safety and security that all women carry within us, a remnant from our cave-women days, where being chosen by someone meant we were going to be taken care of, fed, and sheltered against the elements. It's right up there with our primal need to procreate. As powerful a driver too.

Choosing to be on my own for a time and to not date anyone unless they ticked ALL of the boxes allowed me to see just how much validation and safety I felt in having a man choose me. The degree of triggering to realise this was huge.

You are enough, Carla, even though you are not engaging with a single male on the planet right now, even though no interested man is really showing up for you on your phone or at your doorstep.

You are enough.

And you are safe and secure, my dear inner cave woman, with how life is right now. You don't need to trigger me to go out and seek safety and security in a man. I have my own safety and security. I don't need to find it solely in a man as you did, but thank you for looking out for me. I desire love, connection and laugher, things that life didn't grace you with the opportunity to seek. We've got this.

Life is a mirror to our healed and unhealed parts, and so the beauty and magic of doing the work on ourselves is this: not only does it benefit us, bring us peace and lift our personal vibration, it also in turn magnetises in our life partners who are of the same energetic vibration as us.

Sometimes a big old timeout brings clarity, baby!

It allows us to see the forest beyond the trees.

And it will go on to change the trajectory of your life and your future relationships.

Believe it!

Our Queen Life Path
— what is it?

She's you with your crown firmly on. Like you've never worn it before.

Owning your self-worth, sexually confident in your own skin and body, mastering your energy, choosing consciously for yourself what you desire, seeing your potential and finding yourself a partner that is an energetic, vibrational match for who you are now.

Why do I use this term, Queen Life Path?

Yes, this absolutely is a loving alter ego of you, but it's a powerful one.

If Beyoncé needs a Sasha Fierce persona to put herself on stage in front of hundreds and thousands, you having one to fully own your life path ahead can only be a good thing.

Sometimes when we forget who we are, we really have to throw every part of ourselves into believing in that inner being BEFORE we're feeling it or have even met her.

The people whose energy you admire and love are not better than you, they are simply living life as their fullest self-expression.

Their Queen Life Path is lit up and they're walking it.

Let that sink in. It's not that you can't. It's believing that you can't that's holding you back.

Most people live life a small percentage of who they are. They hold back the parts of themselves that would allow them to shine their own version of magic onto the world.

They stay small. They shy away from showing up in all their magnificence.

The queen or the princess—which is more the essence that you embody and move through life (and love) with?

QUEEN AND PRINCESS ENERGY

Princess

- Compares herself to others and often feels not good enough and tries to hide this. Can tend to change her personality and essence for others. Guarded. Wishes someone would love her for her, not realising she never lets anyone see, feel or taste the real her.
- Moves more from her wounds than she does her heart. She is cautious and closed. She can be needy and seeks attention through her behaviour. He will find her presence initially fun but will feel more drama and a loss of freedom over time because of this type of connection.
- Intuition is often dismissed and drowned out. Not connected with her feminine energy and intuitive gifts. Therefore, she can't trust herself.
- Unsure of her value. Unsure of her worth and seeks reassurance from external validation—desire and attention from others. Does entertain boys.

- Her life path is solely focused on finding a partner or having a partner. The enthusiasm for her life path diminishes entirely when she has a partner.
- Is hooked in by toxic, push/pull and negative behaviours.
- A need to prove her worth, that she is good enough.
- Is more trained in opening herself up physically with someone before she shares her full essence and personality. Not comfortable with being seen. Sex first or early. Soul connection second.

Queen
- Accepts herself and is confident, comfortable in her personality and own skin. Comfortable with being seen as the full essence of herself. No pretence or show.
- Has the space, time and relaxed energy for a good man when he shows up in her life but isn't defined by his presence or lack thereof. He will find her presence nourishing, open, fun and playful.
- Follows and listens to her intuition. High degree of self-trust. A knowingness.
- Owns her value. Knows her worth. Protective of both. Doesn't entertain boys. Boys typically don't try it on.
- Has her own life path going on whether she is single or in a relationship.
- Doesn't concern herself with inconsistency, confusion, push/pull, hot/cold, low-effort nonsense.
- Free in her full sexual expression and energy in spaces where she feels trust and respect. Sex is a means of

deeper connection and expressing herself with another. Sex is not the connection. Wants to be seen and only seeks out those able to see her.

Learning to be the queen of my life has been a journey of finding my confidence, of owning my path, self-expression and worth. It has transformed my life and relationships.

I wasn't always on this path, but I am now.

Now I am in alignment with myself, which allows me to attract into my life everything that aligns with the real me. The highest-self version of me.

I walk my path knowing it is me in my fullest essence, and I expect, trust and know that what is meant for me will come to me on my path.

I don't need to force, manipulate or chase. Something or someone is either meant for me or they are not. And if they are meant for me later, staying true to my path will allow them to circle back for me.

I have my intention, I know where it is I am going, I am conscious of how I want to feel in my life and in myself and my role is to stay beautifully on this path.

Magnetic. Happy.

Living life as my best self.

As rarely distracted from my path as I can manage.

That is all.

Once you find this place within yourself, you never really go back. And you begin to become very good at recognising who or what is taking you away from your life path or who is beautifully adding to it.

Life becomes very clear. Clearer than it's ever been. And your role in it becomes clear, clearer than it's ever been.

Queen energy is the rudder that steers my path. This energy comes completely from within. It has nothing to do with what's on our surface—how we dress or present or what we say.

I am so grateful that the important men in my family and life have always celebrated and encouraged the queen energy in me. Reminded me of this energy when I needed the reminder and further inspired me on this path before I even knew they had.

There is nothing to stop you from starting to live and move through life in this same way. In fact, I wish for you to start now.

I can say, as a thirty-eight-year-old woman who moves primarily with this queen energy (we all carry a little princess on the inside, she never fully leaves us!), that it's defining to have, not just in love but in life.

I wish it for all women.

Ask yourself, what are you not expressing and sharing with the world? What are you not doing in life right now that you should be embracing and running towards with enthusiasm?

What is your Queen Life Path that you're not owning and walking?

This path, when you walk it, will change everything for you.

Why do we avoid fully owning and living our Queen Life Path?

Let's own something outright in this moment. We are the first generation of women to have the privilege and opportunity to be the queen of our own lives with or without a king by our side.

Collectively, this is new for us as women.

And let's extend a little compassion out into the world in this moment too. This change in our dynamic is also new for men.

Both sexes are wondering what to do with this change in balance right now and how it looks.

Men are all levels of WTF and not feeling appreciated for actions and behaviours that were 'enough' in previous generations. And women now want to be loved (not just provided for), to have their own lives, to have opportunities outside of the home and for our growth to be equally supported and encouraged.

But let's be honest here with ourselves too. As women, we may desire this path, but the majority of us are not fully owning it!

What a discord of mixed messaging to the masculine we are sending: *Treat me like a queen, but can you save me like a princess too?*

In previous generations, marriage was as much a transactional exchange as it was a love and family bond—if you were blessed to have that. Someone earnt the income to support the family, typically the man. Someone took care of the home and the children, typically the woman. And that's just how it was.

Now we expect and need both from both sexes. The crossing over of roles has grown and intensified in the last forty years more than ever.

So why do we as women shy away from owning and walking our Queen Life Path enthusiastically and with gusto? Especially when it is so clearly the smartest pathway to lead us out of this current change in the masculine and feminine balance.

Quite simply, we're used to being tied to the kitchen sink and in many ways co-dependent.

We have very few females in previous generations who modelled to us what living our Queen Life path looked like while still having a family and a loving relationship.

Our safety and security, those primal needs again, came almost fully from our roles of caregiver and nurturer within the household. To step outside of those roles in past generations was to be too much and to ask for too much.

Safer for us to stay within the limits of our roles and our place.

We are literally the first in our female lineage to walk our Queen Life Path with this much freedom as we do. I will break many, many years of female conditioning if I can be at my fullest self-expression, loving my life, AND be in a supportive container of a relationship that I've consciously chosen that happily holds and loves all of me.

I was graced with some beautiful great-aunts who I was blessed to know into my teens: Auntie Bea, Auntie Shirl and Aunt Mabel (who I never personally met, but whose tales I heard all about). All were born in the late 1800s to early 1900s and lived well into their nineties. They were gutsy, fiery, beautifully poised women who dressed immaculately and were full of wit, but who chose early on in their life to never marry or have children because of the cost that doing either would have on their life and independence.

They went on to be school headmistresses, work and travel overseas, play golf, live together into their old age, do as they please with their time and keep no man in their life who went past boyfriend or lover—aside from Aunt Mabel, who went on to marry in her sixties.

We don't need to make those same choices and sacrifices as women today to keep our independence and freedom. We get to have it all. Maybe not all at once, but we do get to have it all.

We can have a career and have children. We can have a husband and decide for ourselves if we want to continue working or not outside of the home. Getting married for us does not equal automatically house-bound woman as it did for my great-aunts.

And for this I am grateful. Very grateful.

So, whenever I have had a moment of self-doubt and fear as I've walked my Queen Life Path, whenever I've felt like that elephant again with the small rope tied around my foot, questioning my next step forward, whenever I've slowed down or questioned myself as I've walked along my path, wondering where I'm going or how this is all going to come together for me, I have thought about my great-aunts.

I think about how much they would have loved to be walking and journeying in my shoes. How much they'd have loved the freedom to choose everything they pleased.

Run with it, is what they'd wish for me.

And so I go again, knowing I bring others with me from my past and present when I do.

And so should you, for the women in your family tree who would have loved to be where you are today, doing what you do, with the choices that you have in front of you that they could never have imagined for themselves.

Own your Queen Life Path as much as those ladies in your family tree would love to see you own it.

Women set the tone

A good friend of mine and matchmaker, Louanne Ward, shared this brilliant truism with me one day: 'Women can be taught but they can't be trained. Men can be trained but they can't be taught.'

The statement made me laugh for its political incorrectness but any woman would agree, this feels very much true.

Whether it's a man or woman. What we accept from others in their behaviour is either enabling them or training them to treat us in a certain way.

We are enabling them and allowing them to get away with less-than-ideal behaviour. To stay the same or slowly worsen over time. Or, are we training them on how we want them to be loved, held and appreciated. What we will accept.

Women set the tone.

The boundaries are our own. So are our standards. And when we compromise on these, we are letting men set the tone.

Compromise is a beautiful thing. But not when it comes to the tone of a relationship.

Lift the bar, please, ladies, and keep it there.

Praise and shine light on the behaviour you love— good men want to please us and want to feel needed and appreciated. Give less attention to, turn your back on and don't chase behaviour that isn't deserving of you. Set the tone of your life and relationships knowing that this will either raise the consciousness of your partner or it won't. That's their life path and their journey. Not your own.

Life is a process of levelling up

The job, the relationship, the situation you're leaving is something someone else is manifesting into their life.

Your next is someone else's outgrown. What you're moving on from is someone else's dream. What a wonderful series of sliding doors where we are the only thing that is truly getting in the way of the process.

When we get this, we get life at its essence. We understand its process.

Life truly is a series of up-levels.

When we understand this, we see that the only commonality between the levels is ourselves. It is us that have kept ourselves stuck in the past. And it is us who is doing it in the present moment and into the future.

Living with a Queen Life Path, you levelling up your perception and beliefs about yourself might feel like an entirely new way of thinking and living. And if this is the case, then it might feel uncomfortable at times. Too much, almost.

Welcome to your first up-level of owning what you really want, taking up a little more space than you used to and trusting that everything meant for you will come when it's meant to. Where we desire to go next, what we believe we are worthy of having next all sits ahead of us on the horizon.

A space is always being created for your 'next' to step and evolve into. Life always delivers something else that's wonderful when we move forward with this energy.

Trust and have faith.

Let yourself rise, sister, rise.

Expand brilliantly instead of contracting in your life now.

For those who suffered emotional abuse

If this is you, I want you to know, I see you and hear you more than you know.

And so I ask.

Please stop downplaying the wounds and trauma that taking emotional and toxic blows has inflicted on your soul and spirit. Please stop moving through life as though they're not there. Please stop acting like they're not affecting your future life experiences, beliefs about yourself and choices like they are.

It's a cruel analogy to use but at least when someone punches you in the face, there is no hiding the bruises and trauma they have left you with. You can visually see it. The abuser can't twist it, deny it, turn it back on you or downplay what has just unfolded with words like, 'not a big deal,' 'Why are you still thinking about that?' 'Why aren't you over that already?' or even better, 'I never said that.' It would be there for everyone, including them, to see.

Imagine every emotional blow landing on you as though it had been a physical one. Physical bruises last longer than the moment they're made, so do emotional ones.

If you're experiencing emotional abuse or have experienced it in the past, please don't fall into THEIR behaviour trap of downplaying the deep effect this has had on your soul. Seek professional help.

Please give yourself the same kindness and healing you would gift someone dealing with physical abuse if they were to stand in front of you.

Others may not see your bruises, physically you also can't see them, but that doesn't mean they're not there.

In no way do I intend to downplay physical abuse or domestic violence in this chapter. I intend to only bring light to the emotional abuse people suffer with, often silently, also.

What to expect when you go and change the boundaries on your ex

Know that when changing your boundaries, not everyone is necessarily going to be happy for you.

Stay with it anyway.

And this might apply to your ex now and into the future for a time.

You've changed the rules on him. What you used to accept from him in words, actions and behaviour you no longer need to, have to, or want to.

Changing the rules on someone in regards to how we expect to be treated and spoken to usually elicits:

- A push back
- A 'How dare you treat me, speak to me like this' response
- A 'Who do you think you are?' response
- Further and greater attempts than ever to undermine, control or bully you back into your 'place' where they're used to you being.

This is almost always about control and ego. Throw them some love, light and healing and a shit tonne of compassion. They're adjusting to a new version of you and they don't know how to handle her.

Energetically, they can feel you pulling away even if they don't realise that they do.

Celebrate your personal growth here; you have already risen above where you used to be, even if you're still finding your feet in this new space. Expand into this new place anyway, but do take steps to protect yourself with greater emotional or physical space away from them if you need it. Leave space for the dust to settle and own that, in some way, your behaviour did enable him to be like this, which means that this is simply part of the fallout. A lesson in keeping our standards high, to not lower them and to maintain this tone into our future.

Gift them the opportunity to adjust (or not). Do continue to trust in your own path and self-growth. Continue to value your self-worth.

You've got this, queen, whether they like who you are now or not, agree with it or not.

Self-reflection is often an arse (but we can't avoid it)

I was talking with a girlfriend of mine during our walk while I was writing this book.

She asked me, 'This book you're writing, who is it for?'

I answered, "It's for the woman who has left a long-term relationship and doesn't realise the self-journey ahead of her, who doesn't want to hear about the necessary healing and inner work ahead of her and just wants to dive into her next happily-ever-after relationship."

And she laughed.

And I laughed.

Because both of us, on leaving our marriages, had felt like that too. We both had hoped for the immediate happily ever after story.

We were that woman. Blissfully unaware of what the journey ahead was really going to be about. More interested in finding our next someone who would love us and make it all better.

We left our marriages wanting love and that's what we sought out in the world. Never really thinking too much about the love we needed to seek within ourselves first.

#cliché but true.

Both of us had done 'work' on ourselves leading up to our

marriages ending. But really, looking back, we were asleep to the true healing and self-reflection work that we needed to do on ourselves.

I remember seeing a well-regarded psychic just before leaving my marriage. And like a good psychic, she saw it all. Saw me leaving and was unequivocal in telling me that it was the right thing to do.

And then she looked into my future.

She told me that it would take me five years to meet the right man for me because I had so much growing up and work to do on myself.

When she told me this, I thought, 'Wrong—I can do better than that. It won't take me that long.' And I chose to listen and believe everything else from the reading bar that!

Psychics are often wrong. And I really tried to prove her wrong. Believe me. I did my absolute best.

In those five years, I did grow and evolve as a woman. Even though I hadn't been seeking that journey, it was the journey I walked. I truly stepped into my own as a woman during this time, for the first time ever. And I had several long-term relationships with men who were fully supportive of my growth and journey. Including a marriage proposal.

Relationships that on paper could have been my full stop. One in particular, I assumed was going to be my forever.

Yet I outgrew every one of them. Either I left them or they left me because they knew they couldn't give me what I was ready for.

The heartbreak and loss was real during this time. I was growing and evolving naturally, but I was continually and heartbreakingly outgrowing love along the way.

I knew I was on the right path for me, that I was unfolding and blossoming naturally into my full self simply through the process of living my life. The only thing missing was that love still wasn't in my life in the way I desired.

The self-reflection was deep. Hand on heart, I can tell you that almost every time I didn't want to see the gaps within myself mirrored back to me in such a way. I just wanted to be there already. To be 'healed.'

Whether we ask for it or not, want it or not, the self-reflection will come.

If you're reading this book, you're a conscious, growth-minded and beautiful human soul. And so, self-reflection is going to be part of your journey.

It is divine that you are reading this book. It tells me that you live life more from your heart than you do your head. So many people are the opposite, which is why they find themselves stuck and cycling in situations that feel unfulfilled.

Their logic outweighs their feelings.

Actually, that is the upside-down way to live.

Because your logic can never fully silence how you feel. However much you try.

In life, we should lead from our heart and it is our head that should follow. Not the other way round.

Can you see and feel the different lives that leading with each one brings?

I lived very much from my head during much of my marriage. Leaving my marriage was me beginning to listen and move from my heart again.

My heart was in the driver's seat.

My heart was in the lead.

My head, booted to the passenger's side.

Part of my journey has been learning to trust myself and to trust life in a way that allows my heart to stay open and to lead from that place.

If I could have a conversation with my self straight after she left her marriage. Finally in the driver's seat of her life, feeling like she was going one hundred kilometres an hour but actually going five kilometres an hour with a cocktail in hand, wearing her hot new wardrobe, I would say to her, *Enjoy the journey more.*

I would say, *Stay in your heart and follow your feelings. That's your beauty and what makes you magnetic.*

I would say, *Everything in your own time. Just because it isn't here now doesn't mean it's not on its way.*

I would say, *Trust yourself, girl. Stay always open to life.*

I would say, *Embrace all that life reflects back to you about yourself and seek out a professional to heal yourself.*

I would ask her to take the time to embody everything she has learnt about herself before she throws herself into the next thing or someone.

I would tell her, *Your broken heart is actually your most open heart; let that light shine in when heartbreak happens. That's when the transformation occurs. Don't hide from it.*

Self-reflection after a divorce is an arse. It brings up all the questions and regrets that we sometimes don't want to face and that we perhaps didn't even know were there.

Why didn't I leave sooner?

Why did he leave me?

Why do I fear that happening for me in the future?

What's wrong with me?

All I want you to know is this. Your answers won't all come at once. Your answers will continue to evolve. The layers of the onion will reveal themselves as you live your life. The work is never actually done. It just keeps happening around us.

Let your shields down when life mirrors back to you your wounds and guardedness. Let yourself sit with what this means. Because we all carry these protective shields—it's what we do with them next that matters: lower them or keep them up.

Stay open to getting to know your inner workings more.

Keep doing you.

Heal, don't hide.

The thought of being naked with someone else

It's a block for many women.

And it can be frustrating to feel this way, particularly if our ex is behaving in a way that shows he is free of this kind of thinking and feeling.

Sometimes imagining ourselves naked with someone else is enough to send us back into bed on our own, throwing the covers up and over ourselves.

Too much to even think about.

This is more likely to be true if you were the one who was pushed off the life cliff rather than the one who willingly jumped. There is a certain feeling of safety that comes with one man who we loved being the only one we opened our bodies up to over a long period of time.

The beautiful joy of the sacredness that is being a divine woman. Ours is truly a receiving and letting-in energy—physically and energetically.

The old adage of 'The best way to get over a man is to get under another one' isn't always true here.

I won't lie. Yes, it can sometimes feel like ripping a bandaid off to move on physically like this. It's done. The person we just left or who left us feels cancelled out and we feel empowered—temporarily, anyway.

But the 'temporarily' is the thing.

Everyone's beliefs here are going to look and feel different and that's ok. What's right for one is not necessarily right for another. No judgement here on any woman and how she chooses to move with her body and soul.

But my belief here is that we should only open ourselves up to someone physically when we are truly ready to be seen and truly ready to let someone into our body.

I've had experiences where I have dived into another relationship (or fling) to cancel out the one I just left. Trying to make the process of moving on from him faster!

It never ended well for me.

I ended up in rebound relationships that were not meant for me. And I hurt people in the process.

Men catch feelings too, as easily as women do.

Opening ourselves up to being naked and sensual with our bodies again with another man will bring with it a different timeline for every woman.

There is a big difference between being naked and having sex with a man and being naked and sensually open to a man who is fully enjoying you while you are enjoying them.

This process might look like learning to love your own body for a time because your body is different from the body you had the last time you were dating.

Self-pleasure is important here, especially if you have left a marriage that felt loveless and was lacking in intimacy for quite some time. Especially if you haven't had a full-body orgasm in a long time, whether with your ex or on your own. An orgasm is connected to your level of emotional openness.

So, if you have been in any way emotionally traumatised or repressed, now is the time to explore and deepen into moving yourself out of this.

Embrace your nakedness again and relish in your body for who she is today—have massages, do nude yoga, anything that allows you to connect with your own body and its innate beauty and power.

When you met your ex, quite possibly you were more of a girl. Now you are a woman and your body is ready to be loved, honoured and adored differently.

But that journey starts with you first.

It takes two to be toxic

This can be a bitter pill to swallow.

But I invite you to sit with it because at a point in your life, you chose your partner. No one forced you to be with him. You chose him.

And this means your relationship together was as much a reflection of him as it was you. Whoever might feel more 'wronged' or 'abandoned' in this moment, this statement is still true.

Sorry.

It's not me.

It's not you.

It was us.

When we project our blame onto others, we avoid the necessary process of reflecting on ourselves.

The truth is that it always takes two.

Just like a game of tennis. Someone hits the ball over the net from one side. And someone has to always hit it back. It only stops when someone puts down their racket and refuses to play anymore.

Looking at all the ways we returned the ball over the net to continue allowing this game to play out is powerful.

How someone chooses to show up is their business. How

you show up is yours. Always own yours. Leave others to do as they please with theirs.

If you were hooked on the drama and the push/pull nature, as uncomfortable as it is to admit, own it. If you ignored your intuition and turned a blind eye so you could continue playing this game, own it. If you self-abandoned by downplaying and ignoring your own needs and feelings, own it.

Own it, whatever it was. And consciously choose to do better and different next time. It always takes two for a relationship to be toxic. It couldn't have been a relationship otherwise. You must own your part.

I don't want to be saved by a man, but where do I start saving myself?

The fears I hear.

One privilege of working for over five years with women in this space and season in their life is the commonalities I begin to hear.

The same fears, thoughts and self-doubts that once had you afraid to leave your marriage are also actually the gateway to understanding where you need to save yourself, where you need to feel more safe and secure within.

You've got this, more than you know. As you move forward, inch by inch you will begin proving it to yourself as life falls into place around you.

When we make space and then set an intention, life always responds.

Life stops responding only when we stop.

Facing our deepest fears and limitations, willingly shining a big light on them, is the beginning process of knowing this is where I need to go within, this is what I need to embrace more of.

What I was hearing:
I will struggle financially and completely lose the lifestyle that I love.

What I wish I was hearing:

What a wonderful way to learn to be financially independent and empowered and to create a life that feels as good behind closed doors as it looks. I have time to recreate this lifestyle for myself whether on my own or with someone else in time.

I need to find my own confidence and learnings around money.

What I was hearing:

No one will love me. I won't find love again.

What I wish I was hearing:

I've found loved before, of course I will find love again. This next time will be amazing and more aligned for me than ever.

I need to love and value myself more. I need to appreciate myself more for my own beauty and gifts.

What I was hearing:

This will hurt my children. I am selfish to choose my own happiness over theirs.

What I wish I was hearing:

What a beautiful way to demonstrate to my children what love looks like so they don't end up in a relationship like ours and instead will go on to choose healthier, more loving relationships for themselves. My children learn what love looks like by watching me live my life, not by listening to me.

I need to discover who I am as a woman now—whole, fulfilled, lit up and loving my each and every beautiful day.

What I was hearing:

The grass isn't greener on the other side of the fence. It won't be any better with someone else.

What I wish I was hearing:

I'm using the 'grass isn't greener' line to keep myself safe and I am abandoning my true feelings to do so. What I desire isn't being fulfilled in this relationship. If other people can enjoy relationships and dynamics like I desire, then so can I.

I need to live my life more from a place of honouring my own needs and desires over needing to please others. This doesn't make me selfish or too much. This makes me beautifully human. I move through life from my heart, not from my head.

What I was hearing:

Who will want me or love me with so many children/such young children?

What I wish I was hearing:

The right person will love and welcome my children because he loves me and he won't want to lose me. My children are an extension of me, of course they will be loved.

I need to embrace my children and family as one of the most beautiful parts of me and what I have to offer someone. Family is everything to me and will be the same to any future partner that comes into my life.

I was celibate for twelve months and this is what I learnt

Before this…

I hadn't had a one-night stand since I was nineteen. It just didn't do it for me. I don't judge anyone who does do this.

I was a relationship person. I always found myself in one.

Being celibate for twelve months wasn't something I intentionally set out to do. It just happened, and time just passed. I left a relationship that I thought was going to be my forever and my grandad passed away. Both happening within weeks of one another. The complete pain of losing two big men in my life like that made me do something I'd never had to do before in my life.

I completely stopped.

Two huge pillars of men left my life, and I was lost. Numb. Feeling more alone than ever. Abandoned.

These twelve months showed me how much I was still used to moving from this place of needing to be saved. How daunting it felt to go against this and to cultivate a sense of safety and security for myself. Independent of a man.

For twelve months, if it wasn't a soul that deeply grabbed me, I didn't pursue it.

I came to realise how few true soul-to-soul connections we really do have in our life. How so many of my past ones were more noise than soul. How they had been a distraction from me walking and owning my path. From me owning my strengths, beauty and gifts.

In this time, I became the full creator of my own life. I owned my life path and I walked it solo … for the first time, with no one holding my hand. I found my own safety and security within myself, and realised how much of that I'd received from my grandad in my past. How much I had received from my ex-boyfriend that I'd recently left.

It was so hugely triggering.

But the beauty from this time was profound.

My business almost tripled. My self-growth, confidence and transformation exploded. My self-worth grew. My personal relationships blossomed.

I started swimming and found a new life love.

I had given so much of my own power away because I had shied away from fully owning all of myself. Shied away from being confident and capable on my own. Walking solo for a time finally allowed me to find and embody this. And now I have her back.

I found myself in a completely new space in myself and in my life.

I don't recommend this for everyone. I never place timelines on such things. And there are no things we must do in life.

But for you if this inspires. Create this time for yourself, just like I did. It will open your eyes up to something about yourself.

PART THREE
Your money, Honey

This is going to be a short part of the book, and this is why

I am a single mum who has hustled and worked and evolved herself into being who she is today.

I used to joke to my girlfriends that a smarter woman would have hung in her marriage for another one or two years longer. That would have been the smarter financial decision to make because of all the gains we were finally about to make as a couple.

But there is something about unhappiness, where it goes from being a whisper to a roar—one you can't ignore anymore.

This chapter about money is going to be short.

Not because it's not important. Actually, it's incredibly important.

But because I'm not a financial expert or planner and have zero desire to be.

So I can't tell you what to do here. I can only share with you my story, my journey, my lessons, hoping that something I share will resonate with you.

Financially empowered women have something that women with a lack of finances desire more than anything.

Choice.

And choice, when you have none of it or it's limited, is absolutely, f*king everything.

My money story

I am the eldest child of four. Two brothers and one half-sister.

I am a cruise-ship baby.

My mother was on her first overseas holiday as a nineteen-year-old on the P&O *Fairstar* when she fell accidentally pregnant with me. My dad was a ship steward. He was Portuguese and had recently left the Portuguese army after doing his compulsory time, having been conscripted. He was loving the cruise ship and island life. He also could barely speak any English.

I was named after the black Carla Zampatti dress that my mum was wearing on the night I was conceived. Thigh-high split. Deep V-neck that nearly reached the split. You get the picture. On returning home and discovering that she was pregnant, my mum went back on the same cruise to find Dad and let him know that I was coming into the world—knowing she would find my dad, still being a ship steward and circling the islands of Vanuatu and Fiji.

And just like that, with the aid of an English interpreter, they docked in Sydney and were married straight away for the sake of Dad's visa. My mum was seven months pregnant on her wedding day and no longer able to fit into the Carla Zampatti dress.

They moved into a caravan in my grandparents' backyard in Tasmania while they found their feet financially, and while Dad learnt English so he could find work outside of fruit and vegetable picking.

My parents were married for fourteen years and considering where they started, and what they started with, they did amazing. My childhood was loving.

Dad made lots of Portuguese-speaking friends and life, in my eyes as a child, was good. We lived on three acres, Dad had a hobby vineyard, Mum shopped at the local designer store and was always trying new dishes and expanding her recipe journal.

Looking back over old home videos set to music by the Gypsy Kings and Dire Straits, we were more wog than I realised. It had never occurred to me that not everybody had fresh sardines on their barbecue or bacalhau as a staple dish. Certainly, this wasn't normal for the nineties in Tasmania, in a small town so far from being multicultural that the only Chinese people in town were the ones who owned the Chinese restaurant.

Life was mostly good until my parents divorced when I was fourteen. And before life became mostly good again, for a couple of years it wasn't so much.

My parents' divorce wasn't all that civilised, and through events outside of my own doing and because of choices I made that were best for me at the time, my parents' divorce eventually ended up costing me my relationship with my father.

Despite our best attempts before he died, I never spoke to

my dad properly again without one of us yelling or getting frustrated.

My mum, when she was married, had been the stay-at-home mum and only ever ventured out to work part-time when we were saving as a family to go overseas to visit Dad's family. And that's how I'd always known things.

Dad worked.

Mum stayed at home.

But after my parents' divorce, Dad did the bitter thing—which in no way reflects the man he actually was—and quit his office job at the local paper mill to open Tasmania's first handmade pasta takeaway shop. He started claiming his income at a loss and stopped paying Mum any real child support.

This, among other things, was part of the reason we fell out. I caught Mum crying over the child-support forms one night. So much effort to fill them out, to only claim seven dollars a week from him. I remember her saying to me, you kids eat more than that in one breakfast.

I helped her fill out the forms that night, saying to her if Dad was going to lie about his income, then let him do it.

When Dad found out about this was when he and I really fell out with each other for good. In his eyes, I was like my mum, and honestly I didn't know what he was to me anymore at that time.

My dad was a good man. A beautiful father. And I'm so sorry that he wasn't alive to meet my daughters when they arrived into the world because he would have made a loving grandfather and avô. But this is the story and I have no doubt he'd do things differently if he had his time again.

To get by after her divorce, my mum took on three jobs, waitressing at two different places and cleaning hotel rooms. We went from seeing her all the time to seeing our grandparents and being at their house all the time—thank God for them!

One of the venues that Mum waitressed at held a lot of state functions and events. The menu was fancy. And the kitchen—knowing that Mum was struggling—would keep us all of their uneaten food. We might have been struggling financially during those years of Mum being divorced and single, but we ate like kings and queens on their leftovers. I took quail to school in my lunch box so many times that as an adult I never need to eat another small bird ever again.

My mum was single for two years before meeting my stepdad, Chris, and accidentally falling pregnant to him. And with Chris's entrance into our home and world, a man that was much loved and adored by all of us at the time, life almost returned to how it had been before the divorce.

Mum and Chris pooled their money together to buy a larger house, my mum stumping up more than Chris because of her financial settlement, and Mum gave birth to my half-sister, returning to her role that she loved and thrived in as a stay-at-home mum for all of us.

And life was good again.

She was around all the time again. Our garden was amazing. New recipes and dishes were flying out of the kitchen again and Mum even had time to vacuum the front verandah of our renovated federation home—which lit her up so much that one year we bought her a vacuum that she could wear on her back like a backpack.

I love my mum. And I wouldn't change her for the world. So much of our relationship with money is learnt through observing our parents' experience with it. What did my parents' experience with money teach me? That women struggled financially if they weren't in a relationship.

That men could be selfish and overly protective with their money. That men were better with money than women. That men called the shots with money. That leaving a marriage equalled financial pain.

All of this I learnt as a child without realising it. Can you see how your childhood helped shape your own?

When I hit year twelve in my schooling, I was desperate to have a gap year before starting university. My mum, happily raising my toddler half-sister, declared, 'Absolutely not.' She didn't care what I did but I was to get a degree that would lead me to a job that paid well.

I was so annoyed with my mother at the time but I'm so grateful that she gave me no choice. She wanted me to have the financial choices that she hadn't had. And for that, I'm forever grateful, because she completely changed my life trajectory in doing so.

I did the first year of an arts/psychology degree—hated it and failed it due to my lack of attendance at my philosophy tutorials. I changed degrees and moved interstate, having somehow spun myself a full fee-paying scholarship to the University of Melbourne, where I studied to become a dental hygienist.

I didn't choose that career path because I loved teeth. I chose it because I'd been told that the job paid amazing and there was a shortage of dental hygienists in the workplace. I wanted freedom, I wanted flexibility, and I wanted to get the hell out of Tasmania. So I did.

Thank you to my mum, thank you to the universe, thank you to my life path for delivering me to a career that gave me options and financial stability. Something that not every woman is afforded.

My mum and dad's financial experience certainly shaped my own.

It shaped the career I chose for myself, the man I chose to marry because I could see so much love and financial security in him—not because he had money but because he was good with money. It led me to defer all of our financial plans to him during our marriage because I believed him to know more and be better at it than I, which he was at the time. And my financial story definitely kept me in an unhappy marriage, uncertain whether to leave or not, scared of how much my life would change financially if I ever were to leave.

When I left my marriage and passed through the emotional and triggering car crash that for me was separating our finances, I freaked out.

I left with some money; for that I am very grateful because it gave me choices. But I was also a woman in her mid-thirties who had never been in charge of money on her own before, certainly not in charge successfully.

I still remember standing at the mailbox of my new home after our divorce and opening my first electrical bill. It was the first time as an adult that I'd received a household bill with my name on it solely. Even with money in the bank, I had a mini meltdown realising that for the first time this was all on me to keep up with and on top of.

Money continued to give me anxiety for many years to come. I wasn't sure what to do with it. I enjoyed spending it but felt guilty when I did. And I was forever fond of asking my boyfriends at the time—who, true to my type, were good with and better with money than I—for their feedback and opinions on any financial decision I was making.

Improving my mindset around money and feeling confident with money has been my thing that I have needed to 'save myself' on. And it continues to be. Not because of a lack of it but because of my lower exposure and education to it.

Yes, it has been life changing and important to change the love and types of men I attract into my life. So has been all the self-work I've done to really step into my fullest self-expression and worth. Still, my money journey remains the most important journey in my life that I've taken and continue to take. To own it, improve on it, to empower myself around the topic.

Because ultimately, it was my poor money story that led me to make many of my past decisions in all those other areas of my life.

I find this true for a lot of women. Rather than owning our own financial story and empowerment, we willingly handed it over.

Financial empowerment is less about the dollar amount

that you are earning, less about the dollar amount in your bank—it's all about how much you believe you can earn. And what you do with it when you do.

I'm so proud of myself for over time treading an almost different financial path as a single woman than my mother was able to. And I know she is proud of me too.

Everything she did for me I have made the best of and made it work for me. I am only here because of what she pushed me to do and because of what she showed me accidentally, through living example, not to do.

For that I'm grateful. I have become all that she was and all that she couldn't be. Every generation of women grows financially stronger than the last. I can't wait to see what my daughters do, having brought them up to this next step with me, to start creating their lives from.

Love is rare.
Money is everywhere

Financial fear.

It's the biggest worry I hear spoken about that keeps men and women stuck and in a holding space, afraid to leave a marriage. I can't tell you how many times I've had someone say to me that they would have left years ago if they were in a better financial position, if they didn't stand to lose so much financially.

For women, money equals lifestyle and safety. It is the fear of having to be financially independent on their own, often after having been the lower earner in the relationship.

For men it is the change in lifestyle, yes, but also a loss of perceived self to lose half of their asset pool.

For men, money and what they've built up around them often feels like an extension of themselves, their success. It is often an extension of their ego. It's why a divorce can turn ugly so easily when finances are being discussed; carving up the asset pool is literally like taking a knife to some men's identity.

Love is rare.

Money is everywhere.

I said these words to a coaching client once during a session and they are true.

Do you live more for love and emotional connection? Or do you live more for your money?

One can always be built back up, perhaps jointly with a beautiful new partner one day. One is special when it's found.

Women, if your limitation was your finances, the only way out is to educate yourself and to improve your mindset around your earning potential.

Stop looking to be saved in this area of your life, please.

It is a skill to be learned, not a character flaw. You have it in you. And honestly, if I can learn it, without any real role modelling from women in my family, then so can you.

Do as I did.

Seek out female friends who are clued up when it comes to their finances. Observe how they move through the world financially. How they talk about their financial life choices.

And if you don't have female friends who move through life in this way, then seek out professional services or books for women around this topic.

When we are empowered in this area of our life, our lives change and our choices open up more than they ever have before. It's not about our purchasing power or what hangs in our wardrobe, but what we can say confident and clear yeses and noes too.

This is true empowerment.

You're either a woman with a $3,000 handbag or a woman with a $200 handbag and $2,800 in the bank

I heard this statement at a women's financial event and the words have stuck in my mind ever since. Whether it's a fifty-dollar handbag or a two-hundred-dollar handbag, the differences in both women are quite profound.

I don't judge either woman. I love the three-thousand-dollar handbags. But I don't own one.

And anytime I've ever had a financial win and thought to buy one, I've thought on it and always pulled myself back.

I'm sure that one day I will. But it will come from a place of having everything else absolutely in a line and my finances in excess.

As women, we are sold to every day. Most of us own so much stuff. But the truth is, we don't need as much of it as we think. Not like we feel we do.

Tapping out of the world where shopping made me feel better or more of a confident version of myself, where how I looked and dressed was character defining, has changed me. Changed the kind of man I attract into my world too.

The men around me now are also more financially aware and, dare I say it, grounded.

Not every woman has to be like me, but you can still look good and have money in the bank.

Honestly, I've never valued having money in the bank more than I do now. I'd much rather have it in the bank or in a house, over having it hang in my closet or on my arm.

This has been a real evolution of the way I handle my finances as a woman. A growing up. To embrace the word 'frugal' but to still live an amazing, off-the-show life that is even deeper and more meaningful than before.

To embrace less being absolutely more.

To choose experiences over things.

I move on belongings and items that I no longer wear like a queen and I'm very selective about what I bring in.

This, in my eyes, is smart. And I'm so proud of myself for becoming this woman and continuing to grow into her.

PART FOUR
Finding love the second time around

Whatever you do next, make sure it brings you fun

Whatever kind of love you're ready for next, when you feel ready to start looking, can we agree on one thing together? Let it be something that is fun and that makes you feel good. After everything you've been through, do you really have time and energy for anything or anyone that is draining, hard work or noncommittal?

Did you really go through all you've been through for that?

The answer should be a loud no.

Can we agree on that, please?

I didn't say *I love you* to a man for seven years

There were the increasingly loveless last two years I spent in my marriage where I couldn't bring myself to wear my wedding ring or utter the words, *I love you*.

And then there were the years after I left my marriage. Five to be exact.

Five years of avoiding saying the words *I love you* to a man.

Four of those spent not realising that the word 'love' wasn't even in my vocabulary. Not seeing how deftly I'd avoided using those words in my relationships with men.

If ever there was a stamp of 'I've been hurt and disappointed and I don't want to fully open myself back up to love', this would be it.

I was in a long-term relationship with a man who was also shy to use the L word—beautiful avoidance by me. I was in medium-term relationships with men where I didn't feel the love; it was more of an 'I really like you' situation—beautiful avoidance by me again. And I was in a long-term relationship with a man who accepted and loved me even though I said thank you in reply to his I love yous—avoidance that I still don't know how I got away with for as long as I did.

I was called an ice queen by some of the men I dated who were open to love more than I was. When something is thrown at you more than once like that, it's hard to ignore and make it not about you.

But actually, I was far from an ice queen even though I moved as one in many ways.

At my core, I had always been a softie, a total smoocher and love ball. I was smart, yes, but far more silly than I was serious. Only I wasn't allowing that side to be seen.

Life experiences had clouded that childlike essence in me over the years as I grew into an adult. Dampened her. Diminished her.

Sadly, these men didn't get to experience or see this side of me. Seeing only the occasional glimpse before I put her back into her box.

There is a vulnerability that comes with living as our fullest version of self. To let someone in. For me, being fully seen allowed someone to either love me for all that I was, or not.

Better to not let someone fully see me so that I wasn't on the receiving end of 'or not'.

I was closed to letting love in beyond the surface level. To letting myself love again. It was my biggest, most protective shield of all.

When your safest source of love comes from yourself and not from someone else is when love can never be fully taken away from you again. In this space, an 'or not' from someone else doesn't shatter your entire world. This space is where you find yourself able to let love all the way in again. Where you can trust yourself to love again because you have the deepest love for yourself first before anyone else does for you.

That has been true for me.

Whether someone likes me, loves me or not, it matters very little now. I can still like them and love them regardless. I can still feel safe and loved within myself.

What if you let love all the way in?

For you if this resonates as you journey back into love again.

We don't manifest the end result, we manifest everything in between

This is something many of us forget or don't even realise. That there is an energetic vibration that matches where you are now and an energetic vibration that matches where you want to be. And quite possibly, there's a great difference between those two places and subsequent vibrations.

If you were living in a car, there comes with that a certain energy and vibration, just like there is one that comes with being a millionaire. To move successfully between the two would need to see you manifesting all the necessary steps in between to achieve this. If you were living in a car and I gave you a million dollar mansion to live in you would most likely feel out of place sitting in such a space, believing this was all too good to be true, waiting for it to be taken away from you. And if the millionaire found himself living in a car overnight, he too would feel completely out of place. His energetic vibration being on such a different level that he would look to improve his situation with the tools and knowledge he already had ASAP.

The Universe doesn't gift you what you want. It presents you with the next steps to help you arrive there. It is progressively trying to raise your vibration to the level of what it is that you want. So you can not only have it, but hold it.

This goes for love. Your finances. Your career. Everything.

Everything you have and hold in your life will ascend higher in congruence with your level of growth and your capacity to expand into the energy of being able to hold with love and grace what it is that you seek.

Very rarely do we just make a big leap, and often when we do we find ourselves self-sabotaging our good fortune and without meaning to—much like the lotto winners who within one to two years of winning millions of dollars find themselves broker than they were before and with their most important relationships ruined. Energetically they had neither the skills nor the level of self-worth needed to hold, handle and appreciate that amount of money with grace.

Sending you something you're not an energetic vibration for yet is like pouring water into your hands—it would just slip through.

In love this looks like Mr Perfect arriving at your front door, ready to love and hold you. Would you be ready for him if he entered your life today? Really? Or would you find yourself worrying that he was too good to be true? Waiting for him to leave you, see that you're not good enough or cheat on you?

Whatever we want to come into our future, we need to learn how to become its energetic match first before we can hold it. Closing the gap between where we are now and where we desire to be.

The first step forward towards manifesting anything is always the same. It's small.

Tell me what you want, what you really, really want

You can't get to where you want to be if you don't know where it is that you want to be next.

I'm all for going with the flow of life.

It's how I live my life. I'm very much in flow. In my feminine. And I choose a lifestyle and relationships that support me to live in that way.

But I am always intentional.

I know where I'm going—though I have no real timeline on when it will unfold or expectations on how it will happen. And I know how I want to feel along the way.

A lot of my female clients sit in front of me in our first session and admit this is one of their greatest struggles. To know what they want for themselves as a woman, now. Separate from anyone else's wants in life for them, separate from anyone else's intentions for them.

Beautifully and simply their own.

I like to imagine the elephant from earlier in the book in these moments. Its leg tied by the thinnest of ropes to a stick in the ground. It can go anywhere it desires but it's paralysed from doing so.

So powerful is the mind when it's been conditioned to stay safe in one place, that it can at first struggle to visualise anything different for itself.

In this space, starting small can be everything.

We don't have to have a grand vision of our life right now. We can simply know where we want to be next.

I can't tell you how many times over the last four years that I've wished my journey to finding love and finding myself had been different. So many times. I won't lie to you and say this hasn't brought me moments of sadness. It definitely has.

It wasn't the path I imagined or wanted. But it is the one my soul needed.

The truth is that if I had my time again, I wouldn't wish for anything different to have played out. It's all led me here. To be the woman that I am today. To be the mum that I am today. To be the lover I am today. To be the author and coach I am here today, writing this for you.

The experiences I've had along the way have been magic.

I wouldn't be any of the above things today if I hadn't had the experiences that I have had. In fact, if I'd settled down and stayed with the first partner that I met after leaving my marriage, I would have stayed the same woman I was when I was married.

And there would have been nothing wrong with that, only it's not who I am. Nor was it who I knew I could be.

When my ex-partner broke up with me over the phone while I was moving out of the family home, sending me to the floor of the Alex Hotel shower, he said to me two things. 'You deserve better than what I can give you,' and 'Will you remember me when you're standing on stage one day being the best at what you do?'

I wondered what he was talking about. I saw myself in such a limited, small way then. I had no desire to be on any stage, hadn't even imagined such a thing for myself. A month after we broke up he met someone else, later marrying her and employing her in his business as his secretary/PA ... which had been his ex-wife's job when they'd been married. This was his patterning. And there is nothing wrong with him repeating this patterning if it's what he wants.

Only I was never destined to become someone's secretary. He saw that before I did.

In fact, I think he saw much of my life path ahead of me before I did. My potential, what I was meant for, my gifts, the way I was holding myself back, the language I was using to describe myself at the time—he pointed it all out to me beautifully and then he left, which was as much a gift as the hurt he left me sitting with.

He may not have been the happy ending that I had hoped for at the time, but he remains a poignant moment in my life journey. And poignant moments go on to lend beautiful depth to your life and soul.

Often others can see more of our potential than we can. This is very much true if we feel like that elephant still tied by the smallest of ropes in our minds.

So, I invite you to open your mind up to where you would love to be in twelve months' time. To see yourself through the eyes of potential as others see you.

I'd love for you to think about how you'd love to feel in the next twelve months and to choose one guiding word that resonates deeply for you. Not a goal attached to a person or thing arriving in your life. A feeling. One that will act as your rudder for the next year. Visualise what you could do, achieve and experience in that time that would help you feel more of it in your life.

Your guiding word may change every six to twelve months. My words have varied from vibrant, supported, loved to adored, feminine or free. Every word matched an energetic point in my life at a time where that was the feeling I needed to feel and express.

When we live intentionally from this place of feeling as a woman, we flow with life rather than force life. I liken this to allowing ourselves to be taken with the stream.

We can't fight the flow, we can only go with it and remain mindful of how we want to feel along the way. The touch points we wish to experience as we move through.

This is life. And we can either flow with it gracefully and easefully or we can resist it with control, fear and anxiety.

I go for flow.

I trust the flow of the stream to take me where I need to be; my intention is to simply feel amazing and do my best as I flow with it.

There is fate, there is destiny, there is free will and then there is the magic dance between all three. I believe in all three, though spiritual teachers will tell you that when you're moving with your free will, this is actually you following your destiny.

What is meant for you will never pass you. What and who you need next will always present itself to you.

Choose to know how you want to feel along the way.

Choose to have experiences that will allow you to hold even more of this feeling and energy.

Bloom and blossom in your life enthusiastically.

Balancing our feminine and masculine energies to attract love and true happiness

When I look around, I see many women whose hearts are aching for love, appreciation and support. Who want to attract more of that energy into their world.

Women now have more opportunity, independence and choice than we've ever had before, but many of us are more unfulfilled and disconnected than ever in our personal relationships. We are tired of doing it all or feeling like we are.

My intention is that this chapter will have you questioning everything you have been taught about what it means to embrace your femininity to attract love. That it will help you embrace softness and vulnerability so you can stop living with a guarded heart and the façade of *I'm strong and have it all together.*

My hope is that it will also help you move into a space of flow and away from feeling the need to push or control to make things happen.

I'm so passionate about this topic because I spent so many years cold, closed and in my head. I did not resonate with being feminine at all. I was disconnected from myself and I was unhappy.

Unhappy in myself. Unhappy in my marriage.

For me, leaving my marriage was the catalyst for finally

being honest with myself and with others that while I had been living as though everything was fine, the truth was that everything was not fine and hadn't been for some time.

After my separation, much of my energy was spent on being self-sufficient and independent—necessary life stuff that we all need to embrace as part of the separating process. I was paying the bills on my own for the first time, being Mum, keeping house, working full time and building my business on the side.

I wanted a man but I didn't want to need one. And I was intent on any man coming into my life knowing that. But I was living a half lie, because under the façade I was exhausted and felt so alone. Even though I was dating someone.

At this time in my life, I was completely disconnected from myself and from my feminine. I was living in my head and not from my heart. I was always in my masculine energy of doing and rarely in my feminine energy of being.

THE FEMININE AND MASCULINE OUT OF BALANCE

Wounded feminine
- Afraid to speak her truth
- Lacks self-worth
- Tolerates toxic people
- Seeks external validation
- People pleases
- Apologises for who she is

- Has predominantly negative self-talk
- Compares herself to other women and sees them as competition
- Closed and disconnected from herself and her body

Wounded masculine
- Thinks vulnerability is weakness
- Lives in his head
- Numbs his feelings by focusing on porn, sex, money and power
- Seeks to control and dominate others
- Represses anger and trauma
- Justifies his anger
- Avoidant

What I've come to learn is how important it is for women to embrace more of their feminine energy in its healthy, unwounded form. How much more fulfilled and centred we feel on the inside when we live and move from that place. How it changes everything that we attract into our world when we do.

The love we attract. The friends we keep. The lifestyles we live. Literally everything changes.

All women are both with an innate feminine essence and energy, trusting, loving, soft, playful and vulnerable.

Simply, life and the experiences we have had since have made us otherwise.

All of us carry both masculine and feminine energies. It's important to know that the balance of masculine and feminine varies in all of us. All of us move between the two depending on the task we're knee-deep in or what is on our mind at the time. So, we do need to learn to dance between these two energies successfully in our everyday life.

This energy shapes who we are attracted to, how we perceive each other, and what we draw into our lives.

Which of the four predominant energies do you move through life with at your core? The healthy or unhealthy masculine? The healthy or unhealthy feminine?

THE FEMININE AND MASCULINE IN BALANCE

Divine feminine
- Honours her truth, her feelings and speaks it
- Knows her worth
- Sets loving boundaries
- Feels validated from within
- Inspires others to shine
- Lives unapologetically
- Speaks gently to herself
- Embodies her divine goddess and encourages other women to rise with her
- Intimacy killer: Feeling unseen, unsafe or misunderstood. A man who creates a push/pull energy in their relationship.

Divine masculine
- Lives in his heart

- Doesn't fear vulnerability
- Embraces his feelings and his strengths
- Communicates clearly
- Seeks to understand himself and others
- Makes big things feel small
- Honours both the masculine and feminine energies
- Takes responsibility for his actions
- Intimacy killer: Being criticised, controlled or shut out. A woman not in touch with herself.

Since the beginning of feminism, both men and women have rejected aspects of their masculinity or femininity to avoid being perceived as dependent and helpless or macho, respectively.

I had disowned aspects of my feminine self because I saw embracing them as weak and an invitation for a man to hurt me again. I was much more comfortable and confident in being seen in my masculine persona—strong, together, independent and capable.

Heaven help the guy who was dating me at the time and just wanted to love me and be there for me unconditionally … he didn't stand a chance!

In this masculine space, I pushed people away who didn't deserve to be pushed away, and for a time I attracted men who were emotionally unavailable, who didn't know what they wanted or who weren't relationship-ready. It was this experience that made me start to reflect on how I was moving through the world and acknowledge that maybe it said as much about me as it did them.

Damn that!

I realised that in being so independent, I was attracting men into my space who were actually being respectful of and admired my independence. They had no desire to impede on what I had going on or to be there for me— that was part of the attraction for them. They liked that I was so overly independent and together. It told them energetically that I wasn't looking for a man to fully show up for me.

I had it sorted, or at least I acted like I did.

I want you to imagine for a moment a seesaw with each side equalling fifty per cent when in balance. The two together always having to equal one-hundred per cent. I realised I was overly in my masculine space and out of balance, sitting high up on the top of the seesaw; let's just say I was eighty per cent showing up in my masculine energy, so most of the time. It meant any man who chose to sit on the lower end of the seesaw had to be comfortable only being twenty per cent in his masculine; he would need to be more in his feminine energy to want to sit there.

While teetering on the top of my seesaw, I realised several things. I wasn't moving through life as the woman I wanted to be and knew I could be—I was tired of doing it all, the sex was lacklustre up there, connections and love with others never felt genuine and deep, and on top of it all I felt like a fake, behaving like I was all good when I wasn't. I was lonely and tired. I was tired of being go-go-go all the time. I felt far from peaceful and at ease in myself. And I came to realise that I needed to lower my side of the seesaw closer down to fifty per cent to allow and make space for the masculine man I knew was a true match for who I was on the inside.

I had to let my walls and my defences down.

And as I did, dropping into and embracing more of my feminine side and energy, the men I started to attract, who started to show up and take a seat on the other side of the seesaw, started to change. Men in a healthy masculine place who knew what they wanted, who were respectful, who wanted to see me happy and fulfilled now had space to sit down and were choosing to sit down and stay on the seesaw.

The other men I used to attract—the unavailable, the emotionally wounded who needed saving or were just looking for sex—stopped approaching me altogether or I wasn't interested in them.

Why is it important that we get to this place if we want love and happiness?

Because we want a life and love that fills up our cup over one that empties it. For women, this is when we feel our most content—we feel loved for all the wild parts of us, heard and safe. We have more spirit and energy when we're in this place of balanced feminine energy on the seesaw. And men sitting in front of us in their balanced masculine energy feel their full selves—appreciated, needed and free.

A woman living in her feminine energy longs to connect with what's around her. She wants relationship. She thrives on being more than she does doing. She wants love and to be loved.

I have a well-developed masculine energy—I love to

succeed in my business and be the driver, and I enjoy life when I accomplish my goals. However, my deepest longing is for intimate relationships and connection. Life without those two things might look successful on the outside but it would feel empty on the inside.

When I was honest with myself and got out of my own masculine way, admitting without shame what was missing in my life, I began to invite it in. I learnt to be predominantly in my feminine energy in my life. And I learnt how to be in my masculine energy when life needed it from me to achieve and get things done. Most importantly, I learnt to park that energy when I was done.

So how do we embrace living more in our feminine energy within a busy world? A world that often supports and needs us to be more in our masculine—succeeding and earning, thinking more over feeling, hiding over letting someone in to love us again?

How to drop into and embrace our feminine energy

One of the hardest pills to swallow after leaving my marriage was realising just how much I'd been in my masculine energy during our relationship.

I won't deny that he did cause some amount of it with his behaviour, but I did a beautiful job of perpetuating it also. I can see how I co-created our dynamic and enabled it to continue as it did. I can see how I added to our coming undone as a couple.

Being in my masculine was definitely me in the energy of being Mum and getting everything done. It was also a self-protective mechanism I used to shield my heart from some of the more hurtful dynamics present in my marriage.

I'm sharing this in case you've come to realise this about yourself after reading the previous chapter—that you spent much of your last relationship in your masculine or wounded energy too. And I want to say to you, me too. And I want to let you know that this 'me too' is true for many women.

Hindsight's a bitch sometimes when we see that life has left us with results that can't be undone quickly like we wish they could.

This is living. This is living a beautiful journey of learning along the way. Embrace that truth and be kind to yourself.

There are no mistakes in life. Only lessons. Take the lessons always and run with them.

1. Create a life that supports the feminine.

All of us have parts of our life that require us to operate from a driven, results-based and focused masculine space. Often this part of our life pays the bills and is our achieving side—like our career. It can also be the energy that keeps the house going and ensures the children are at all of their after-school activities week to week.

To prioritise the feminine, we need to bring more balance outside of those hours to support us in embracing and falling back into more of a feminine energy as often as we can.

Cultivating and choosing to be in relationships that allow us to show up in our healthy feminine—warm, safe, intimate, where there is trust and respect—is important here.

From my years of coaching women and from my personal experience, I can share that it is a challenge to be in our healthy feminine if our relationships are attacking, cruel, abusive or lacking in affection. In fact, if our relationships are abusive, it can sometimes be unsafe to be in our feminine energy more than our masculine.

Adding more behaviours into our day—whether at the start, during our lunch break, or at the end of our day—that energetically move us back into our feminine is everything. This will move us from being in our head and place us back into our heart energy—where a feminine woman mostly moves from.

Getting into the fresh air and sunshine, sitting with the peace of it all, journaling, free-flowing types of exercise like yoga or Pilates that energetically unwind us, freeform dance, and grounding our feet in the sand, grass or water are all wonderful practices. Literally anything that takes you out of your head and returns your attention into your heart space.

Changing up how we dress outside of our careers can also be a great way to delineate between work self and feminine self—this might mean choosing softer colours, styles or cuts that speak to you in a feminine way outside of your nine to five.

2. Breathe life into your feminine in moments during the day.

When we're too much in our head and acting from a place of thought, the feminine starts to feel drained, worn out, frayed and exhausted. This normally happens when we're in our masculine making decisions, analysing, planning, organising and over-thinking.

A beautiful, discreet way to connect with our feminine during the day is to send our attention to the area in our womb space and disengage from our mind. I love to do this while walking. I focus my energy on that area and breathe down into my lower belly while softening my shoulders, heart and throat. You will find your walk will change slightly when you do this, your hips will soften and even take on a slight sway. Or if we're seated, we can simply take a moment to sit and breathe deeply while focusing our attention on the area in our womb space and disengaging from our mind.

When you start playing with this practice, you will notice that men around you start to notice the shift in your energy!

I experimented with this in the past with an ex-partner of mine. I found when I was in my head, he was less likely to touch me for no reason. But when I moved my focus to my womb space, I softened immediately and he responded, coming closer for no reason, touching for no reason. It was like a moth to a flame! He sought out my energy and warmth without realising he was.

In your career and your everyday, taking moments like this will leave you feeling more connected and refreshed and, if you love the work that you do, purposeful.

Another beautiful and discreet way to bring subtle attention to your womb space in your day is to carry a yoni egg inside you. (Please seek advice from a professional therapist before use if you've never used a yoni egg before.)

Explore this technique. You will be pleasantly surprised!

3. Being Vulnerable.

Vulnerability is not an invitation to air all of your dirty laundry or to post your every emotion on social media! Vulnerability isn't being needy.

Vulnerability is sharing who we are with others—the real self underneath the façade—and to show up freely as her.

Being vulnerable is a necessary part of opening up to love, connection and passion. A healthy masculine energy has a natural desire to protect and provide for the feminine. He wants to feel the vulnerability and beauty deep inside of you.

A woman who can embrace her own feminine energy, her own feminine strengths, will allow the space for a man to provide and care for her. And she will have more ease and joy in her relationships with men as a result.

A woman who always has her everything-is-perfect façade on is not as deeply attractive to a healthy masculine man because he will feel unable to fully connect with her.

One of the qualities healthy masculine men seek the most in an intimate relationship is that of a woman's warmth. Men are attracted to warm, friendly, open women they can relax with. This is different from 'easy' or 'easy to please' women. Very different—so please don't confuse the two!

Often women consider themselves warm and open when, in reality, they are only like that around their close friends.

Whether you can be as freely yourself with a man as you are with your closest girlfriends is a beautiful barometer of where you are on this vulnerability scale.

Are you the same person with your friends as you are with love interests? But please keep in mind here … not all men are deserving of this presence and energy from you. Steer yourself into a healthier feminine space and steer yourself towards healthy masculine men that know how to adore and appreciate you.

4. Releasing the need to control the outcome.

There is a beautiful paradox in life that exists for all of us—when we give up control, we in turn actually gain more freedom, power and relaxation on our path towards true happiness than we ever thought possible.

Going with the flow is such a cliché, I know. I prefer to think of it as flowing with and seeing things as they are now over how we need them to be.

Letting go and trusting the timing of life, trusting that others show up as best they know how when we leave them to their own devices, trusting that this approach creates space for true happiness in the long term, even if things don't evolve or eventuate as we wish, is a test for many of us to maintain.

Our ego loves to feel a sense of control over the outcome. But it's an entirely false sense of control.

Living with a sense of flow is accepting that we have no real control and that everything happens when it does and of its own accord.

In love, this means if we want a man in our life who loves us, then we allow him the space to show us that he does. We don't step into the space and do the work for him.

We give him both the space and the opportunity to do this himself.

So many of us struggle with leaving this space because we're trying to control the outcome. We over-analyse, fall into anxiety, grow impatient and end up just doing it ourselves to close the space. Why do we do this? Often it is because of the feeling of uncertainty it brings to leave that space empty and waiting.

We tie up an awful lot of our self-worth, self-love and abandonment issues into that space and how quickly that space is closed. It's one of the biggest challenges I have with clients: to relax their need and compulsion to manipulate, cajole or bring about a certain result.

Tony Robbins says it best: 'The quality of your life is in direct proportion to the amount of uncertainty you can comfortably deal with.'

Self-awareness and the ability to regulate ourselves in positive ways is everything here. As is understanding why we're doing this and to take a deep breath and distract ourselves before we do something to close the silence and the uncertainty.

For me, embracing my feminine energy and choosing a life and relationship that supports living as this woman has completely opened up my world. It has changed my life. It has expanded me.

I could never return to the woman I used to be, I could never tolerate or attract some of the things that I used to in my past relationships. I'm too soft and playful in my intimate relationships and too open a person for that now.

I would never allow someone into my space who could ruin that energy in me now.

This is the space I wish to see you in too.

To find that curious, soft feminine energy within you, and to protect it like the queen you are.

A woman only has room for one king in her heart

The king in your heart should be your partner. That makes sense if you're the queen.

But for this little girl, the king in my heart had always been my grandad.

When my dad left my life when I was fourteen, pushed out mostly by me, my grandad stepped straight in.

And all of a sudden, I found this kindred spirit within him.

He started driving me around in his little two-seater van, full of machinery and train equipment in the back, taking me to all the places he needed and wanted to visit.

God I had some of the best times and conversations in my life in that car. He'd pick me up for an hour and I'd be gone all day. And I never minded.

We talked all the way. He'd tell me about our ancestors, our family tree, what I came from. He'd tell me stories about his life, sometimes he'd ask about mine.

When he passed away, it was a soul-shattering blow to my heart, like it was to many in my family and in his social circle. He was on a pedestal in my mind and I had no desire to topple him down. And honestly, in my world, he deserved to be up there.

When he passed, it was like a big seat was left sitting

empty at the table in my heart. And I naturally looked to my partner at the time, someone I'd been in a serious relationship with for eighteen months, to take that seat for me. It wasn't a conversation that we had, more it was just an energetic change and shift in me towards him.

For the first time in my womanly life, I actually needed a man to be something of a deep emotional support for me. I needed a king. Not a prince.

Four weeks after my grandad passed away, after having a necessary conversation with my partner at the time about what I meant to him, this partner of mine ghosted me and refused to see or speak with me ever again.

It felt like two deaths in the space of one month.

The man who had always been my king and the main man in my life, and the man who I had thought was going to be that man for me next, both gone just like that.

I was crushed on more levels than I knew possible.

On the surface he had shown up for me like a king but actually he turned out to be the biggest prince I had ever known.

I literally went from waking to his 'good morning' text or phone call every morning, seeing him most nights of the week, hearing from him at different times of the day, always getting a goodnight from him whether in person or on the phone, to nothing. Zilch. Nada. Nothing. Like I'd never existed to him or mattered.

It was like someone had snuck up behind me and pulled the rug out from under my feet.

I spent much of that year not knowing who I was grieving

for. I was numb. My feelings were so intense and in so much of a mess. Was it my grandad I was grieving for? Or was it my ex-partner? Hoping and assuming always that it was more my grandad because at least he deserved it.

A woman only has room for one king in her heart and mine had always been my grandad, and when I realised this, I realised something else. This meant I'd only ever had room for a prince to come sit down at the table in my heart. The king seat had already been taken in a very solid way.

No one had ever really compared to my grandad in my eyes and I'd deliberately chosen princes that could never have possibly filled or threatened his seat. Princes that didn't even want to.

If you're the apple of your father's eye or a daddy's girl, this might be why you've chosen princes for yourself too. This may even be stopping you from fully stepping into your highest self, your own version of a queen self.

When I realised that I'd never wanted to topple my grandfather from his pedestal, I saw all the ways that my choices had kept him up there.

My grandad was the safest source of love from a man in my life. Every princess needs a king to look after her and he was mine.

I wish I'd learnt this before he passed. In many ways, my grandad passing was the invitation for me to become my own version of a queen and start my journey to becoming an energetic match to the now-empty king seat at my table. To step out of the princess seat I'd sat in so lovingly next to my grandfather, shuffle along the table and claim my new seat.

And to then patiently keep living my life while I waited for someone to sit down in the empty seat beside me.

If my grandad passing was the invitation to step into my queen seat and life path, my ex-partner ghosting me was the push.

The following years' lessons after my grandad's passing were difficult because of the loss, but they have become increasingly graceful because of the personal gain.

Before he passed, I talked about my sadness over this to him—that I could feel I was entering an exciting new beginning and season in my life but that he wasn't going to be here to witness it.

I feel a certain serendipity and a passing of the baton in the fact that the end of my grandad's life overlapped with a new beginning in mine.

Within four weeks of his passing, everything that wasn't meant for me or good enough for me walked itself out of my life. From my career through to my love life. The shit took itself out while I watched, slowly falling to my knees in disbelief. Everything I had thought was certain in my life, I discovered was not.

I truly believe it was all of my grandfather's design. A complete clearing and reshuffle of my life table that brought me, in many ways, to write this book. I'm grateful for all of it now.

A woman only has room for one king in her life, just like a king only has room for one queen.

Make sure you have your seats filled right.

The three stages of love in a woman's life

No men were harmed in the making of this journey through the three stages of love ... but I do want to acknowledge them for their gifts to me in my life. If we parted because of my actions, I'm sorry. If we parted due to yours, thank you. You leaving me was a gift.

Many of us know at least one or two couples who chose right the first time. They've been together forever, are an absolute image of what love looks like even with their ups and downs. They're couple goals.

The truth is that for most of us, coming to that sort of love is a journey. For some of us, it's a short one—we learn the lessons a little slower, our childhood conditioning is something we need to overcome as we unwittingly recreate our parents' marriage dynamics in our own lives. We get stuck in wound-mate relationships that keep us trapped in certain stages, or some of us simply tap out of relationships entirely because we just don't want to get hurt again.

If it gives you any assurance at all, know that I was the latter. A slow learner, fond of getting myself stuck and eager to repeat my mistakes!

David Deida describes three stages of love a woman goes

through in her journey to loving and honouring herself before being able to fully experience a true loving connection and relationship. I recall experiences and relationships in my life where I moved through these stages myself. And I've found these same experiences to be true for many of my clients.

There is no easy ticket through the first two stages of love, and if you're reading this book, this is most likely where you were. It takes practice, self-awareness and a commitment to honour our desires through our choices instead of pretending they don't exist. And that is a frightening concept for many of us—to feel sadness and loss at what we don't have, to acknowledge what is missing that would light our life up.

I see so many men and women shut themselves off from feeling into their desire to be in an extraordinary relationship because the prospect is too painful. They don't want to be disappointed or hurt again, they feel safer when they don't expect too much or anything at all from love.

Rather than remaining stuck in one of the first two stages of love, I'd love for you to ask yourself instead—*What do I need to do to grow into the next stage of love?* And when you have your answer, do that.

Be patient with yourself through these three stages. Don't try to rush yourself through them or pretend you are further ahead if you are not. Life is a journey and success is finding joy in the process not just in the result.

Stage One

'I need to get the love from someone else'
— A wound-mate relationship

Most women's first attempt to get the love, appreciation and feeling of self-worth they need, so they feel whole and enough, comes from a man choosing them over them loving themselves first.

I certainly did this.

I looked to men for much of my self-worth, my answers, my certainty, the direction I was taking in my life and my validation of being good enough. When I look back, I can see I yearned for love because I lacked appreciation for myself, and in order to stay in some relationships I chose to ignore and downplay some behaviours and my needs.

Most women can resonate with some or all of that sentiment at one time or another. Many of us fear the loss of love in this stage as though we are at risk of not finding it ever again in another man. This fear is how we can find ourselves stuck here.

In this space, we rarely make great choices in who we attract into our life. And whether this relationship lasts a lifetime or a short time, there eventually comes a time when a woman wakes from her 'happily ever after' dream and realises through her own unhappiness and dissatisfaction that this isn't a true match for who she is. And that she cannot rely on or look to another to give her the love and appreciation she needs from herself.

In this first stage of love, I moulded myself into a version of the person my partner needed me to be and I pushed aside my intuition in order to stay in relationships.

Breaking free of this stage saw me having to acknowledge my pain and dissatisfaction over pretending it didn't hurt so badly. And like a pendulum that has been pulled too far to one side before being finally let go, I swung with vigour straight over to the opposite side, propelling myself into the second stage of my journey in love.

Stage Two

'I don't need anyone else because I am capable on my own so this needs to be an equal relationship'
— A wound-mate relationship

When a woman is in this phase, whether single or in a relationship, you will find her working on herself and her personal growth. You will find her trying to find or rediscover herself. She is strong and self-sufficient, at least she appears and presents herself in this way. This was the time when I wholeheartedly embraced my masculine side and became more economically and emotionally self-sufficient than I ever had before as a woman. I started giving myself the love I had been trying to get from someone else. And I wanted to be in a position where I felt like I had it all together for myself and for my kids. Strong, secure, safe.

I didn't want to find myself needing anyone again. Instead, it had to be a partnership of equals. One of wanting a man over needing a man.

This was a better place for me to be in. It broke my previous patterns of always needing to be in a relationship, of getting over one relationship by getting straight into another one, of defining myself by the man who was in my life.

I found myself and discovered who I was as an adult woman in this second stage of love. It was an incredibly empowering stage for me.

But at the same time, I also had an energetic wall that guarded my heart. I struggled to truly let someone into my world. To truly feel safe and open. To let someone love me and see all the sides of me.

I mostly maintained a façade of 'everything is fine and I am strong/capable/empowered' in this stage. But I also didn't have love and intimate relationships that were deeply fulfilling and connected.

Women in this second stage often fall into one of two ponds. They seek out sex to feel desired, for attention, for sexual needs' sake or for the mini ego stroke it gives them so they can feel like they still have it going on! Or they do the exact opposite, closing off from sex almost entirely—their sex drive dropping or disappearing in the process.

If a woman in this second phase is in a relationship, it will be with a greater expectation of equality. She will expect her mate to support her career as much as she does his, to respect her time and energy as much as she does his, to support her decisions as much as she does his. He'll have time for himself and she will expect the same time in return to indulge in her own thing.

On paper, this second stage might read close to perfect.

But if we are in a relationship that aligns with this stage, it often, over time, starts to feel like it is missing something. And it is almost always a true, deep intimacy and sexual connection that is lacking.

The level of emotional depth and connection can feel not enough. In truth, we can only witness and love someone as deep as we are able to witness and love ourselves.

Stage Three

'Love is unlimited'
— Open for a soul-mate relationship

When a woman is in this phase, she no longer feels the need to guard her heart anymore. When something or someone hurts her, she stays open. When she is hurting, she stays open even if she wants to close. Love has expanded here from what she needs to get, to what can she give.

This does not mean that she allows herself to be taken advantage of, or that she gives more than she receives. It doesn't mean she has no boundaries for toxic people that invade her space. She is love and she doesn't forget herself— it's how she moves through life.

She puts her own oxygen mask on and she keeps it there before she puts anyone else's on.

A woman in this third stage relates to others in the world around her with love because her cup is already full. She is not guarded. Her presence opens up others. Her energy warms and fulfils others without taking any away from her.

David Deida calls the leap from the second to the third stage 'the feminine crisis'. We reach the third stage with an open, unguarded heart and we start dating, only to be subsequently hurt or triggered, and without realising it, we return to the second stage of love to lick our wounds, heal and find ourselves again.

Our heart opens. Then it closes. Opens again. Closes.

When we do this, we don't allow ourselves to meet our pain head-on and move through to the other side. We resist it. We repeat our old patterns that we had previously thought healed.

Yet, if we can allow the pain and heartbreak to open us and sit with us, something wonderful happens. We return to love and we are filled with love.

Looking back, I see what an enormous signal I put out to the universe of my need to be so independent because I'd been so hurt. And the price I paid for such safety which kept me from the intimate relationship I actually desired.

Through my pain, I opened my heart, and the way I love has never been the same again.

Things feel much worse before they get better—know that's often the case. But we must have the courage to break through and reach the other side. When heartache comes, say, 'In time, I always move on from it better and brighter.' Or even, 'Every relationship is more aligned and truer for me than the last.' When disappointment comes, refuse to close your heart, because tomorrow is always a new day.

These are the mantras of a woman who has her own back, who is love and who is open for love. Whose love for herself is enough—she does not need the love of another to fill any void.

When we embody this kind of loving, love shows up differently for us and our relationships flourish. And they will flourish because we will know that love, as long as we remain open for it, will always come back to us in bigger and more beautiful ways. With full trust in ourselves that we will bounce back brighter each time, even if love disappoints.

Everything magic that will happen to you will of its own magic

We can't micromanage the universe. But gosh, we sometimes like to try! Timing, outcomes and what someone is thinking and feeling … good luck trying to control any aspect of that.

It is simply futile.

I've learnt some beautiful life lessons, and continue to, around staying in the present moment and living with a sense of detachment to the outcome. On trusting the timing of my life. On walking with hands wide open to the experience of life over hands tightly gripped onto people and things in an attempt to force them into being or staying a certain way.

These lessons have cleared my energy and lightened the load that everyday living can sometimes place on our shoulders. And I wanted to share them with you.

1. Let your life unravel forward in front of you.

I don't hold on to what's no longer working or bringing me happiness. I believe this is a powerful technique in avoiding the mess because my hands are not clasped on to having anything remaining or staying a certain way. I try to always stay open. This means if it's not meant for me, there's no deep resistance from me. I let it go.

2. I follow the breadcrumbs in my life.

What's the obvious next step? Spirit signs. My intuition. The magic synchronicities and meant-to-bes that happen in life. I'm open to all of them speaking to me and take them as positive signs, breadcrumbs leading me down the path of my life. I follow them.

This includes those times when my life path asks me to leave my comfort zone. Trust and have faith in the next step.

3. Don't avoid the avoidable.

Usually it's not hard to recognise when someone or something is no longer for us. It's just sometimes hard to accept. I don't choose to ignore what I want to ignore and see only what I want to see. I try to always witness things how they are.

4. It's important to not place meanings on things but it's important to still notice the signs.

I try not to read between the lines or make assumptions. If it's an 'I don't know' or an 'I don't know why', I let it remain so until life shows me the answer. I don't try to close that space and uncertainty by creating a story for myself. I heal my anxiety over the lack of an answer with something else— exercise or reading, or catching up with friends.

To me, this is living in flow and alignment with yourself and your life. This is flowing down stream rather than fighting to hold it together in one place, forcing things to happen at a certain time or in a certain way for you.

Maybe what is meant for you is better than what you've ever imagined happening for you. Why would we get in the way of that unfolding for us? There's a thought!

If you pay attention to the patterns of your life and look back on the ones of the past, you'll realise that everything always works out. Everything always takes you to a greater destination next. You always grow, and the things you think you can't survive you somehow get through. That's the beauty of life. Always remember that.

Tell me when leaving one thing didn't take you on to something else even more amazing and aligned for you next?

Never!

Your job is not to pave the path in front of you, but to keep facing your true north and to take one step forward after another on that path.

Things are not going to work out the way you are planning—how beautifully exciting.

There are no shoulds—how freeing.

Have faith and keep showing up because everything will work out even better than you could possibly imagine when you let go.

Come what may. Stay what may.

Believe me.

Choosing from your worth over choosing from your wounds

There's a big difference between choosing a relationship from our worth and choosing one from our wound.

When we choose from our wound, we miss the red flags without realising we are. We ignore our intuition, we self-abandon continuously to maintain these relationships, and ultimately we are seeking out someone to heal us and love us as proof of us being good enough.

Many of us are becoming more and more (delightfully) conscious about our choices and discerning about who and what we let into our hearts and bodies. This is amazing and will in time level up the connections and consciousness between all of us.

Now is really the time to become more self-aware than ever about this concept of wounds and begin to unravel and ask, what are mine?

Often, we continuously attract people into our life who represent healing for us. Healing that needs to happen through addressing unresolved lessons from our past, so we can move on.

We're experiencing an unhealed wound from our past in the present moment when life or someone triggers us. It is essentially an open wound and subconsciously we are seeking out this next person who we hope will give us a new, happier ending and the healing our soul needs and seeks.

When we choose from our wounds, it looks like:
- Rushing into and defining a relationship based on honeymoon hormones
- Choosing based on a fear of being alone
- Wanting to be loved to feel 'good enough'
- Feeling validated by someone having chosen us
- Abandoning our needs to keep the peace and maintain the relationship by not acknowledging and following how we really feel or what we really desire from another

When we choose from our worth, it looks like:
- Taking our time and not rushing
- Qualifying our values: Does this person move through life in a way that aligns with me and supports me?
- Asking: Do we share common paths to build a relationship and life together that will celebrate us both?

Moving into a place of our highest self, where we feel the best we've ever felt inside and out, is truly the place where we can begin to draw higher levels of magic into our lives. In our relationships, our careers, pay cheque and friendships.

In fact, our whole personal vibration lightens, lifts and brightens the more we are on our Queen Life Path, moving and choosing from a place of worth over our wounds.

With every relationship you enter into in your future, I

would love for you to ask yourself, *Is this relationship creating safety for my wounded self or is it a beautiful container for my highest self?*

Every relationship we choose for ourselves should ideally be one that holds us in our highest self-energy or one that inspires us to be in that energy more.

When I let people love me, they ...

Please finish this sentence in your mind.

What was the first word or words that came to mind for you? The first answer that comes immediately to mind is almost always the right one.

Our answer to the question, *When I let people love me, they...* says so much about our beliefs, expectations and conditioning around love. This is a representation of a core wound we need to heal and move you through.

When I let people love me, they ... leave me. Why do you believe this? Who was the first person to really leave you?

When I let people love me, they ... hurt me. Why do you believe this? Who was the first person who taught you that loving someone also meant you would be hurt?

There are many varied answers to this question: use me, take advantage of me, lie to me, betray me, think they own me. Our answer simply highlights our past experiences with love. And unless your answer is something along the lines of, *When I let people love me, they love and adore me*, then it's something we need to heal and explore.

For as long as we believe something, we will manifest it. Our beliefs are self-perpetuating, and through our choices we validate our perception of the world.

Change these and we change our results.

When I let people love me, they love me back.

When I let people love me, they love and adore me.

When I let people love me, they can't help but fall in love with me.

When I let people love me, they stay.

Whichever resonates for you (or a version of your own, of course), she deserves to be written on your bathroom mirror in red lipstick for a time until you feel it in your body to be true and meant for you.

Who is going to be a good container for you now?

Who is going to be a good container for me now? I asked myself this early in 2020 when I decided to step back into dating after choosing to stay out of the dating space for a time to heal and level up what I was attracting.

I see so many men and women in this washing-machine cycle of dating. Jumping back into the dating pool over and over the same person they were before and hoping for a different result.

Typically, all that happens is we attract a guy who is the same shade of shit as the one we just left!

So when I started looking around again, when I opened myself up and declared I was ready, I found myself surprised with what I attracted and who I was attracted to.

The time out I'd given myself to do me, heal me, had changed everything.

The same kinds of guys showed up for me as they had in the past. They were motivated, smart, driven, a family guy, a little bit wounded and picking up the pieces of their lives and hearts.

Old Carla, who had last been single almost three years ago, would have happily dated these men to see where it might have gone. She would have seen their potential. How they ticked almost every single box except maybe one or two important ones. She would have made it work.

But instead, I discovered that what used to land for me in a man didn't anymore. And the man who I would have described as my type in the past, who would have happily have chosen me—I could see I wasn't landing for him either.

For a few months, I lamented that I had never had such a terrible strike rate when it came to dating! Nothing was landing for me! I felt like Happy Gilmore trying to putt the golf ball into the hole, what should have been an easy last shot—every shot just kept skipping across!

I realised my type had changed.

I was, to use a phrase often used to describe women in a negative way, 'too much' for my old type. My new-found confidence I could see made him question his. My new-found sense of self-worth made him question his.

My relaxed nature and feeling of openness and sensuality that I had discovered in myself for the first real time as a woman made him feel less than.

My outer walls and constraints were gone. And I could see that not all men were comfortable holding such an energy or knew what to do with it. And so I sat back and asked myself the question of *Who is going to be a good container for me now?* Who can I be my full self with without having to diminish or downplay parts of myself? Who can stand beside me, hold space and let me be me, with my full inner light on, no mask, no shield. Completely me in my feminine, living beautifully.

Just me. All my sides. My desires. Wounds. Glories. Stupid stories.

Who is comfortable enough in themselves that they can be that container for me? Who seeks out a woman like me?

I want you to know: No feminine woman is ever too much for a man. She's just asking him to have more presence, self-assurance and strength in himself than he currently has to be able to hold her.

You are not too much. Energetically, he knows he's not enough.

Who is going to be a good container for you now that you own your worth more than you ever did before?

Explore this, because what you need now is most likely going to be very different from anything you've ever needed in a man before.

How to know what you are vibrationally aligned for

Noticing how things are turning out for you is one really clear way of understanding which Vibrational requests you are emanating, because you always get the essence of what you are thinking about, whether you want it or not.
— Esther Hicks, Jerry Hicks

I've learnt there's what we say we desire and then there's where we actually spend all of our time, attention and thought. Sometimes even our money.

There's what we say is important to us and then there's what we actually think about, desire and crave.

This so often explains the phenomenon of what we say we want not showing up for us. It is our often subconscious, rather than our conscious mind, that presents us with results in our life.

We say we want love, but actually the majority of our time and focus is on our careers and financial independence. So our careers blossom.

We say to ourselves that our career is important to us, but actually our eye is looking for love, connection and laughter. So love and the other sex show up.

There's no right or wrong. There is just the season that

you're in and whether it's aligned with what it is you truly want.

There's just what is showing up for us (or not) and asking ourselves, *Is this what I really want?*

I can't tell you how many times I lamented and felt frustrated in the past with what was showing up for me. But if I actually looked at where my time was being spent, where my attention was going, the truth was that my results always made complete sense.

My side business struggled at its initial stages because I was in the season where all I really wanted to do was go out with my friends and socialise. My time went there, my focus was on organising my social calendar. I wanted to find love, I found that. The side business came second, third even.

Where focus goes, results flow.

Sometimes we just have to honour the season we really are in, knowing it's not going forever but it is where I need to be right now, and throw ourselves into it with full attention and excitement.

It's often so beautiful what shows up for us when we're happily focused on the season we're truly in.

The magic of serendipity, where what's meant for us arrives in our life of its own magic and accord.

There is what we attract into our lives and there is what we let in

As you begin to move through the dating world, I would love for you to know this.

You are not wounded, broken or flawed simply because you keep attracting the same kinds of people and situations into your life. Can we please drop the guilt, shame and 'I'm still not healed enough/good enough' narrative to explain this phenomenon?

The truth is that if you're an empathetic, attractive, caring, catch of a woman with a heartbeat, then you're going to attract into your life all sorts of men who desire your presence and energy.

Instead of seeing everything that presents itself in life as a mirror of what we are not doing right, can we ask instead …

What am I saying yes to and what am I saying no to?

What am I choosing to let into my space?

So often it's more about what we're choosing than it is what we're attracting into our life.

If I were to put you into a room full of beautiful conscious men who were ready and open for love, would you be drawn to them? Or would you still find yourself drawn to the guy in the corner who's wounded, not quite ready or not good for you?

Only you know the answer to this question!

If you're still saying yes to controlling men, narcissists, cheaters, people who bring drama, unavailable men, low-effort men, then there's not necessarily anything wrong or broken with you.

You're just not owning your worth or value enough.

Crown on again, please, queen.

Yes, what you attract speaks loudly about your own healing. But also, what can we do to raise your worth in your own eyes? To raise your value in your eyes?

Knowing what we actually deserve and moving with this energy is everything and it's as much about your no's and your yeses as it is what you attract in your life.

Every time you say no to something that isn't serving you, it creates space. It builds your self-worth. It realigns you with your intentions, goals and desires.

Your no is one of your most powerful signs to the universe that you know what you deserve. It's you saying *Don't bring me any more of that* and *Please deliver me what I deserve when the time is right.*

Use it!

The only important thing you need to know when you are ready for love again

There is so much love, dating and healing advice out there in the world. And it is mostly all wonderful and good advice too.

But as with anything, sometimes too much is just too much. It begins to feel confusing.

When I was pregnant with my first daughter, I did the first-time-mum thing and read all the baby books. So when I had my daughter, I had all these well-meaning ideas about how feeding and sleep times should look. And I was all over the leap years and milestones too.

My mum was supportive but found the whole process of my learning to mother quite amusing and very different to her own.

One day she said to me, 'You have so much information available to you now that we never had, but actually, parenting you three kids was easier without it.'

I feel like dating and the healing journey is maybe nearing this point of information overload.

It is all deeply necessary work for everyone. In no way am I suggesting it is not.

But if I could give you only one piece of dating advice that I feel everyone must know at this point in their life, and tie it up with a pretty bow for you, it would be this: The wounded masculine is afraid of commitment, and the wounded feminine tries to force love.

See this and you see the push/pull of woundedness that exists in both marriages and in the dating world. The feminine trying to convince, cajole and manipulate the masculine to commit and stay. The masculine who pulls away, self-sabotaging and self-abandoning too.

Remembering, of course, that we all carry masculine and feminine energies inside us, which means you can be a woman who is shy of commitment or a man who is trying to force love. We wear both energetic shoes.

I have been both these energies. The woman in her wounded feminine who tried to make a man love her more and stay. And the woman in her wounded masculine who pulled away every time a relationship became too intimate or someone loved a little too close.

Being both has taught me this. When we meet someone in either space, we only need to accept them for where they are now. We risk our hearts and our sanity when we expect or hope they will change for us.

This doesn't mean your love wasn't enough. Only that they weren't in the right place to appreciate it.

We can't love someone's wounds away, as much as we might want to try. We can only love away our own.

Go where you can be loved right.

This is us moving through life with our hands beautifully open instead of gripped and holding on to an outcome. Observing. Eyes open. Self-trusting. Allowing others to be who they are, not who we want them to be.

The work is not in learning how to fix a wounded masculine or feminine energy in others. The work is in healing our own energy and staying beautifully on our own Queen Life Path.

If a man wants to join you, trust me, he will, and with very little effort from you.

Stop trying to love the wounds out of someone else.

Love them out of you instead.

So where are all the conscious men?

Where are all the conscious, divine, single men doing the work on themselves?

I hear this question (or complaint that there are none) from women all of the time.

They're out there. I know because I meet them and I have clients who meet them.

The question is more, are you a conscious, beautiful, self-loving woman who is doing the work on herself?

Ask yourself honestly. Would a conscious, beautiful man who is doing the work on himself be attracted to you right now? Are you someone who this man would be drawn to? Are your choices aligning with this energy?

We first have to become an energetic match for what we want to attract into our life. Every time this is true.

We can only ever attract and hold in our life what we're ready for—our own point of attraction. Every time this is true. Very rarely is it a true lack of something existing in the world. Instead, it is the lens we view the world and ourselves through.

Women may complain that many men are only after one thing, that they're noncommittal, emotionally unavailable and wounded.

But men complain too. They complain that there are many women out there who need saving but expect to be respected and treated as though they don't. They have anxiety, trust issues, they're not financially independent (I don't mean wealthy, I just mean independent), they date around, they're needy or they need constant validation.

There are always two sides to every coin and I find women can be very adept at projecting onto the masculine what they're not doing well. Entirely overlooking what they as a woman could be doing a little better themselves.

If you want to be treated like a queen, then you need to show up as one. Men energetically pick up on princesses who need saving. A prince will be drawn to this energy, a king will not.

I want to end this chapter by sharing a truth here that exists for both sexes.

We do not need to be fully healed to be in a good relationship. There is no such thing. In fact, a beautiful relationship can be one of the most healing experiences we are blessed to enjoy in our lifetime.

Life is a never-ending classroom. It isn't a classroom where, once given an A plus, you get to leave because the learning is done. It is a forever classroom.

Finding love and meeting a wonderful someone is also not the end of your learning nor a reason to leave the classroom, though many people like to take it as such.

Ultimately, what both sexes desire at a root level, from this place of self, is to connect with someone who is an active participant in the classroom. Someone who is happily fulfilled in their life path and doing the necessary work to move themselves through life, ideally alongside someone who is deeply aligned with them.

The world needs more conscious divine men, yes. But it needs more conscious divine women too.

Women, stop your hunting, you're not good at it

He's not for everyone I know, but I love some of Steve Harvey's work and his thoughts on dating and the dynamic between men and women.

It does align with how I choose to move through the world. It doesn't have to for you. Each to their own. I believe his approach does align with our innate biology as men and women and with our more divine masculine and feminine energies.

In his words, 'Women, take yourself out of the hunting business because it's not what you do. Men are hunters. We hunt all day. That's what we do. Stop your hunting. You're not good at it.'

In my own personal and professional experience, I have found this to be almost always true. When a man knows what he wants, he will make himself known to you. He might do it in a loud, more pronounced way, or he might do it in a more mild-mannered way. Either way, he will make himself known to you, he will put himself in your path in some way.

I believe it's not a woman's job to hunt down men. It's my experience that when we do, we end up inadvertently hunting the wrong kinds of men for us. Often the ones we regret having ever met.

I know this chapter might sound entirely politically incorrect in a world where women are rightly given much the same opportunities as men. But most of us have experienced this at one time or another, when a man knows what he wants he rarely hesitates long to try and capture it. In fact, he will often go out of his way to make it happen.

And let's be honest with ourselves, ladies. When a man is like this, when he does, it's next-level hot and sexy.

I only want a man who knows what he wants. I have no desire to capture a man and convince him that he wants me. I believe every woman should love with this energy.

In every consensual, reciprocal, romantic exchange I've had with a man, if I've felt him hunting me and I've decided I like the look and energy of him, then I've slowed down just enough to let him know that I was open to his hunting and made it just that little, little bit easier for him to start a conversation with me. Whatever that first interaction might have been.

For most women, this is true. We very subtly help out the guys we like!

Even as I move into dating a guy, I mostly still do keep that same energy. A man hasn't 'captured' us just because we said yes to talking to him or going on a date with him. In my mind, I'm still weighing him up and deciding if I like him— the decision isn't his.

I see and coach too many women that fall for a guy simply because he chose them and gave them attention. No! It's not about that.

What about how much you really like him? What about if

he's good enough for you or not?

So if it's more of the man's role to be the hunter, where does it leave us? To stand there and look pretty? Waiting like prey? No.

It's to be on our Queen Life Path. To be happy and content in ourselves, wrapped up in doing our own thing, open for love when it comes, looking and feeling good and enjoying our own life in the best possible way.

It is a man's job to place himself on our path and keep himself there. Not our job to drag him onto it and hold him there.

Men do value what they need to chase and work for a little. I'm not at all telling you to be manipulative or play games. I am suggesting that you let him put in the thought and effort to plan, *How am I going to approach this woman? How am I going to put myself on her path until she notices me enough? How can I not lose the attention of this hot piece?*

And it's for you to not merge your energy with his so early, just because he's given you some attention—you don't know enough about him yet!

Dismiss this chapter entirely if it doesn't align with your beliefs, but I'm a big believer in this approach.

Are they really emotionally unavailable or are they just not that into you?

Emotional unavailability. It's a term that is thrown about a lot.

There are definitely emotionally unavailable people in the world. Absolutely.

But.

I feel it's used to the point of overuse sometimes.

There are a lot of labels out there for men in the dating world right now—narcissistic, toxic, emotionally unavailable.

But if we dig deep enough, what we might also see are our own ego tricks here. Our ego trying and doing its best to keep our personality and self safe from rejection and perceived criticism by making it about them and not us.

I know that this can initially make us feel a little defensive, but stay with me, please!

I'm going to make a broad generalisation, but there are generally two types of men out there in the dating world.

The first is the man who is excited to meet the one. He's ready. This man is always honest and upfront about what he's looking for. He doesn't hesitate to show a woman who he is interested in or what he thinks and feels about her. These men are sure about what they want.

The second type of man is still focused on building (or rebuilding) his career, his life, his financial standing, and isn't looking to invite a queen into his castle just yet. He isn't looking for that distraction. This guy is almost always honest and upfront about his needs from the start too. In his words and in his behaviour. He may fall in love with a woman during this time, yes. But only if he meets a true match and feels that this woman can contribute to building his castle. And if this happens, then he won't hesitate to show her how he thinks and feels about her.

How often do we as women encounter this second type of man, and instead of taking him at his words or actions, fall into thinking, *I'll change his mind* or *He'll change how he feels for me.*

I see women do this all the time.

All the time.

So I guess what I'm asking you here is to consider if he really was emotionally unavailable. Or was it more that he was not looking for a relationship? Or maybe he was just not that into you?

If we hadn't put as much effort and time into these relationships, would some of them have lasted as long as they did? Some might not have even really started or got off the ground if we hadn't made ourselves so available.

Something for us to ponder on as women—the ways in which we enabled the relationship to persist even though it didn't truly meet all of our needs.

I'm yet to meet anyone who doesn't come with some degree of baggage. Myself included. Even after years of self-work and reflection and journeying through all of it, I still carry baggage in my backpack.

We all have our triggers.

I do believe that we as women need to stop alienating and criticising the masculine as much as we do. We do ourselves and them no favours. One sex is not more evolved or better than the other.

Just because men don't communicate or move through the world like we think they should, that doesn't make us right, it just makes us different.

Many labels we project onto men to explain away their treatment or rejection of us are just that. Projections. Projections that might be protecting us from fully having to sit with truths that hurt to admit, our own role in things unfolding as they did.

I'm not making excuses for men here at all. Ghosting, disappearing, pulling away and not communicating emotions is immature and uncaring behaviour. But can we please realise that we as women are better practised at expressing and feeling into our emotions than men? Our conditioning has supported us to connect with our feelings and our emotions since we were little girls. Most men did not have that same experience and conditioning to cry and express their feelings as little boys. So they do show up and move through the world in different ways than we.

Boys are so often conditioned to get back out there and keep on playing when they cry. Most have been conditioned to simply soldier on.

And men have learnt it's safer around women to not share their truth and their feelings so they don't hurt or offend us. This is true as much as you might think it's not.

How often do we ask for a man's opinion or true feelings only to feel hurt or hold on to their answer as ammunition forever and ever, amen, because it wasn't what we wanted to hear?

So often.

As a result, many men have learnt to stop short of sharing their truth and their feelings with the feminine. An attempt to avoid hurting our feelings or avoid the emotional outburst that it may cause.

There are fewer narcissists and emotionally unavailable men in the world than there are great humans just muddying their way through life in the best way they know how.

The less we look to label someone, the more we are able to see someone for their similarities. A human being. Doing their best in the best way they know how.

Red flags and men who stick licorice bullets up their arse and eat them

I'll get to the licorice bullets in a moment.

But first, let's talk about red flags and how much we sometimes love to ignore them. How much we do our best to try to love these red flags away.

There are red flags we see from the moment we meet someone, but choose to overlook. And then there are those red flags that don't present themselves until we've known someone a little more intimately over time.

Some quirks are such bright red flags flapping violently in the wind, from the start, that they simply must be acknowledged.

Don't downplay those ones!

So often when a relationship ends, it's because of differences in values, behaviours and character that we ignored and downplayed in the beginnings of the relationship as not a big deal. Experience has shown me that what we ignore and downplay doesn't just persist, it grows exponentially over time. The one degree of difference between two people's values at the start of a relationship becomes twenty degrees of separation after ten years together.

I know this has been very true for me in some of my past relationships, where the reasons for us breaking up were the same things that we'd been disagreeing on from the start.

The discord never really went away.

The way they used to speak to me and treat me. Differences in the bedroom. The way we loved to spend our free time. Red flags and deal breakers look different for everyone.

If there's one thing that I've learnt during my 'Seconds Please' journey of finding love after my divorce, it's that it takes longer to truly get to know someone later in life than it did in my twenties when I was dating. There are children dynamics to understand. Exes to think about. Everyone is a little more set in their nuances and ways. And yes, some of those things might be undone and change over time, but some of those behaviours are just the way they will stay.

A bit like our licorice-bullets-up-the-arse man as experienced by one of my clients. Yes, he liked to stick licorice bullets up his arse and eat them. On his own and as foreplay.

This guy was absolute perfection on paper when they first met. He literally ticked all of the boxes. I remember her saying to me, 'I can't believe this happened to me so easily,' and it felt very much like that … until they jumped into the bedroom and an innocent chat about their sexual desires and preferences produced a chocolate-covered red flag.

One untick against the sexually compatible box on the ideal-guy checklist overrode every tick still left remaining as a positive against his name.

Some things you just can't work with or compromise on.

Some things are there to stay.

Don't compromise on your personal values and integrity to keep a relationship in your life. I'd have saved myself much heartbreak if I'd taken that approach much earlier on than I did.

Make a call on it.

Early.

Stop trying to love away those red flags.

How long should we wait before defining a new relationship?

The first ninety days when you first meet a man are more for observing him than they are for falling in love with him and defining a relationship.

I know.

Carla of the past was very quick to put on the rose-coloured love glasses very early on too. The trouble was, I then missed some of the obvious red flags and saw a man's potential over who he was now and who he was probably going to remain.

In those first ninety days, before we get our hearts set on someone, we're first looking to see if he even inspires us to stay in his energy. This is not about him choosing us. Why do we give men this power? It's whether we want to choose him. Is he deserving of you? Is he consistent? Is he loving? Is he able to go deeper and get more intimate? Is he aligned with you and your values? How does he navigate pressure and what does he do with discomfort when you're disappointed in him? Is the connection growing over this time?

Because if it's not growing, it's dying.

That's the first ninety days.

This still allows for feeling love-at-first-sight emotions, but just allows you a little space to also see if someone is worth falling into.

With this way of moving, we're not waiting on someone to choose us, we're weighing up and deciding if we want them to be on our Queen Life Path with us.

Are they going to stay on our life path with ease or with our constant effort?

I always go with ease.

If you are someone who needs to define a relationship early, before you really know someone ... why? Is it clarity? Is it safety? Is it so you know where you stand? Is it because of your excitement at feeling chosen by someone?

These are all wonderful, beautiful things to feel but they can also cloud our intuition and our logic.

The truth is, when we're in a loving, fulfilling, growing relationship that is flowing naturally, it just is. It doesn't need to be defined.

You know already that you're important.

What I am suggesting is that it's never a good start when we feel that we need to define a relationship, particularly in the first ninety days. By nature of flow, it should feel defined in itself organically as we continue getting to know someone.

For some reason, we are feeling insecure about our place in his heart. Is it because of how he's showing up for us, or is this a reflection of our emotional selves? It is always an invitation, when we are feeling insecure in this way, to first find more safety, security and validation from within ourselves.

With love to you on this one.

It's a universal struggle for many women and falls very much into our primal need to feel safe and secure because we've been chosen by someone.

In this modern age, we can choose ourselves first and be just as safe and secure. We can be in the early stages of getting to know someone without having to define anything and still feel safe and secure.

What to do with low-effort men and why they trigger a 'try harder' response

I could make this chapter really short for you and just say: do very little with these men. But I'm going to elaborate for you!

Men are simple. We like to make men out to be more complicated than they are because as women we like to talk, and this veers so very easily into talking too much about ourselves, analysing our life and relationships to the point of creating stories and assumptions about the situation. Ones that often don't quite match the reality.

Men are simple.

Low effort is low effort.

And if low effort is triggering an 'I need to try harder response' from you, then I'm going to come right out and say something. This tells me that first and foremost, you are probably not owning or understanding your own value or worth.

Effort needs to increase as the relationship evolves, not decrease—a simple truth we often forget when someone has hooked us in but then only gives us enough to keep us there.

We don't have to earn effort or work for it.

But sometimes, for some reason, we seem to like to. As though working for it somehow means he likes us more.

Actually, it's the opposite.

The less we have to work for his attention, the more he actually likes us.

Read that sentence again, please, if you need to.

Low-effort behaviour actually triggers in us two wounded responses that make us feel we need to try harder to capture their love and attention.

Our abandonment wound kicks in—the fear of others leaving us. This is usually conditioned into us as children through our childhood experiences and then reconfirmed through our adult ones. If you're reading this book, then you've most likely left a marriage and long-term relationship whether by choice or consequence. It's quite probable that you have an abandonment wound, to some degree, as a result.

And our self-abandonment wound kicks in—all the ways we abandon and don't honour ourselves. Downplaying our feelings, acting against them. Continuing to chase and pursue a man even though his behaviour makes us feel terrible about ourselves is a classic form of self-abandonment, to give you an example here.

You, my dear, are worth all the effort and then some.

And I'm going to remind you again, because it's so important and clear a sentence!

The less we have to work for his love and attention, the more he actually likes us.

No one needs to work that hard to be loved. Certainly not you.

Healing our own needs, mothering ourselves over abandoning our needs is the healing work here. Stop outsourcing that to a man who you are still getting to know and who is still getting to know you.

Future tripping and how we sometimes create our own pain

Ladies. Can we please acknowledge that sometimes we cause much of our own pain when we do this: When we go future tripping on ourselves.

Whether we've gone from first date in real life to marrying him in our head straight away because he is so perfect, and the date went so well. To holding on to what may now be an outdated dream, where it started off so well between you both and now, you're holding on, hoping it will get back to how it was.

Releasing imagined futures and our need for them is one of the hugest clarifiers you will ever have in your relationships. All of a sudden, how someone is—rather than how we want them to be—now becomes vastly apparent.

Let your man show up beautifully for you in the now— or not if he's not doing that.

Yes, everyone has potential. But can we just acknowledge how hard it is to inspire and motivate ourselves to change and show up for ourselves? How impossible it is to try to inspire someone else! Particularly if they're not open or ready.

Release your imagined future and story. It's all make-believe. Instead ask … are you enjoying the now with him? Does the now feel delicious and fun and giving between you both? Is he showing you that he's interested? Is he bringing out the best in you?

And stay always on your own Queen Life Path, focusing only on your next few steps ahead.

If he's meant to be in your future, let him be, but don't go writing the script out for him just yet.

Leaning back in love
and what it is

Leaning back is the antidote for those times when a man pulls away—whether it's just him seeking out his own space or because he's just not that interested.

So often, when a man pulls away, I see women leaning in even more in an attempt to call him back into her space—reaching out, calling, stalking them on social media. If you've had any experience with males like this, you would probably know that doing any of this actually has the opposite result to what you want; they end up pulling away even more.

Men are wired so differently than us. In so many ways. I can't even explain it other than to say that they are. What we need is not necessarily what they need.

Our partners are not actually responsible for helping us to manage our emotions, anxieties or moods … we are. I wish more women were aware of this, the impossible task we place on our partner's shoulders to carry both themselves and us.

Queens regulate their own nervous systems.

So if something feels off in our nervous system, this is when we should be leaning back from him and leaning more into ourselves. Our self-love, our life, our hobbies, our pursuits, and our passions that light us up. All the ways that enable us to settle our nervous system.

It is a leaning back into ourselves that raises our vibration, because we are doing a very queenly thing. We are not making anyone else responsible for our feelings or ourselves.

We're regulating our own feelings.

When things are going well in a relationship, when there is natural flow and give and take, when it feels good, then there is no need to lean back.

Leaning back in love is something that we do when things are feeling clunky in a relationship or dating situation, when things are not in flow, when we're questioning their effort or intentions, when we're not sure where we stand.

Leaning back is us removing some energy. Us removing some access.

Being less available.

Being less accessible.

And putting all of our attention back on ourselves.

This isn't us playing games, this is us taking space because we need it, because we're not sure how they're making us feel, because we're feeling off.

And this is us fixing how we feel for ourselves. Not to get a response or change of behaviour out of them.

Leaning back is the subtle art of leading from behind as a woman. It is not manipulation. Leaning back is a beautiful way to own your standards without leading with your demands.

For many women, leaning back feels and sounds counterintuitive. Men pull away and instinctively many women feel the need to lean in more. To close the silence or to close the space with some form of connection that reassures her. But for men, it is the opposite.

While we may seek connection, men actually desire freedom. Not from us, not freedom to cheat or treat us badly, just to feel a sense of it in their lives. This is how men fill their cups.

Why do you think you see so many men out in the water, surfing, but never really catching all that many waves—just out there on the water? This is them taking space to recharge energetically.

Being able to lean back and take your own space when you can sense that he has pulled back shows a comfort and quiet confidence in what you have to offer. And a trust that if he's not the right match, there will be another one.

How he responds to you leaning back, how he shows up on his return, highlights how invested he is in getting to know you more and keep you in his space.

Leaning back is vulnerability. It's loving and investing in another with open hands.

It is the process of letting go of attachments and leaning back into self.

It's us not giving our value away based on how someone treats us—which means that, for some of us, we first need to see our own value more.

And if we lean back and we don't like their response (or lack of response), this is your loving reminder that this isn't the invitation for you to do more. It is the invitation for you to do less for him and to do more for yourself.

God, I wish I'd known this sooner.

Be patient:
miracles take longer
than settling does

If you think you're settling, you almost always are.

Finding peace in the journey has been one of my biggest life lessons since leaving my marriage. I was always so results focused. So impatient! And it really took away from me being able to enjoy the process and the evolving of myself and of my life.

My desire to be somewhere other than where I was, for something to be more than it was, often led to me settling. At the time, I felt it was better to have something than to have nothing.

When we stop settling is when we can truly call in what we deserve.

In fact, every time we settle, it reinforces that little part inside of us that wonders if we're good enough.

You are capable of calling in more. Just because you haven't experienced the ease, love and life you wish for in the past doesn't mean it won't exist for you in the future.

There is no need for anyone in life to settle for anything less than what they deserve and what lights them up.

Timing is everything.

Magic is real.

Be patient.

The serendipitous nature of our lives is truly beautiful when we allow and believe in this energy of what is meant for us always finding us. Living life with open hands rather than ones that are gripping on, trying to control outcomes, allows what's meant for us to walk in with ease and what's not to walk out with equal ease.

The heartbreak that cracked me open, that led me to be the woman ready to write this book, all came about because I continued to settle in my life and in love.

Learning to not settle, to wait patiently for magic to happen to me has been my life-path lesson in love.

There's no more bitter pill to swallow than to break up with someone after eighteen months together, realising if I'd only stayed broken up with him at the six-month mark (when we first broke up for the same reasons), instead of chasing him back, I wouldn't be here in this position.

There is no need to settle.

Be patient. Leave the space open for everything you truly want and deserve. Live your life path happily until what's meant for you presents itself.

It's on its way. My life is proof of that.

I am only here today because I finally stopped settling.

Everyone is a ten out of ten to someone

I once had a boyfriend where on the second time I slept over at his house, I woke to a surprise.

He had kitted out my side of the bathroom with the toiletries he thought I might need. Toothbrush, toothpaste, face wipes, hair ties and a hair brush. He'd even put the hair dryer out.

No one had ever gone to such an effort for me so early on before. When I thanked him for it, I said my typical female statement at the time, 'Oh, you didn't have to do that for me.'

And his reply taught me a great lesson about men.

'Yes, I did. You're a ten out of ten to me, I want you here visiting me at mine.'

Had there been other women stay over at his house in the past who were not a ten out of ten for him? Yes. Had they received the same full toiletry service as I had? No.

When men find in you what they desire in a woman, and when they're ready for it, they will go out of their way for you. They will put themselves on your life path and make themselves needed and wanted on there.

Everyone is a ten out of ten to someone. For every woman that needs a man, there's a man that needs you too.

You don't have to be a perfect version of anything to be

a ten out of ten to someone. There is no need to compare yourself to anyone—your looks, your body, your age, they are all irrelevant. How you are today is a ten out of ten to someone. Trust me.

Maybe he's not in your existing social circle—expand your social circle, be active in living your life or use online dating.

There is a ten out of ten out there for everyone.

You just haven't run into yours yet.

Go where you're seen and appreciated for what you are.

A ten out of ten.

The person who is your one will probably be quite different from the one you imagined

It took a dark night of the soul for me to realise that everything I once thought was good for me and a perfect match for me, was never really that at all.

It was never about the one and finding the one. Well, it was. Only the one turned out to be someone I never realised it was going to be.

Me.

When we start moving through life at our fullest self-expression is when we are able to call in what's aligned for us.

It took me five years post my divorce to find myself living in my fullest self-expression and to fully step into that energy. To step into her in every moment. To really own her. Exude her in every one of my cells whether the people around me liked me, approved of me or not.

It took so much undoing and shedding of old skins to finally find myself in this place.

The people whose energy you admire and like are not better than you, they are simply people out in the world, living life as their fullest self-expression.

Let that sink in and silence the 'I'm not good enough' voice of yours on the inside.

Most people move through life living at a percentage of

who they are. They hold back from the world the parts of themselves that would allow them to shine their own version of magic. That would allow others to love and adore them completely.

When you are freely this woman on the outside as much as you are on the inside, then it's going to happen for you. The person who is going to be your one, he will arrive. And he is probably going to be someone quite different from what you could imagine for yourself right now.

His age. His lifestyle. His quirks, social status, career. You won't know what's a beautiful match for you until you reach that amazing vibrational space of knowing who you are in a different way than you ever have before and living as her.

I know it's going to look so different for you than you could ever expect now. And I know that when you reach that person and space, you wouldn't wish it to have happened any other way.

Queen Life Path, ladies.

Keep going.

And enjoy the many pots of gold you're going to discover along the way.

Eventually, you will get to this point

Eventually, you will get to this point where men walk themselves out if they know they're not good enough for you.

Your energy, your vibration becomes so clear that the 'wrong' men will know energetically that they're not going to be enough to hold you or that you deserve more than they are willing to give you.

When a man walks himself out like this, don't fight him on it.

If he feels he's not enough for you, then this is almost always the case.

And it's not because you're too much. You're just on different energetic levels.

In this space, you're going to need and deserve a dreamboat of a man who is sure of himself, certain in what he can give you, wants to watch you blossom in your life and who thrives around your energy—emotionally, physically and sexually. You will light up their life with your joy, fun and passion.

That guy won't walk himself out on you. He'll find every reason he can to stick around.

Wait for him.

Serendipity and allowing for more of this magic in our life

Serendipity ~ (n) finding something
good without looking for it.

My favourite life energy.

Those magic life moments that come together on their own. That make you stop and think *Wow* at the brilliance of life.

I allow so much space for serendipity in my life. I force nothing. I move with less attachment now than ever.

I've talked a lot about living with this energy throughout this book for a reason. It's life and soul changing.

I observe and let life unfold in front of me. I stay present.

How do we allow more serendipity to happen to us in life?

- We show up as our best in this present moment and follow this pattern of energy every day
- Let go of our attachment to how things must be or happen
- Accept others for who they are over seeing them for who they could be
- Have faith and trust in the process, even in the mess

- Stay on our life path, one that brings us enjoyment and fulfilment
- Move through life with hands that are open, allowing what is meant for us to stay of its own desire and what is not to slip through

And how do we hinder this magic of serendipity?
- We allow ourselves to fall into doubt and too much future thinking
- We stay attached to the idea of how things must continue or look in our lives
- Have set timelines on when something should happen for us
- Force or manipulate things to happen in certain ways, which is us playing with and delaying our life path, a path that would have otherwise unfolded naturally in front of us
- We move through life with hands that grip and resist letting go of those things no longer working, feeling good or meant for us
- We overthink and ignore our intuition and the pathway that is happening for us

Keep the magic of serendipity alive in your life path.
Let go.
Serendipity exists in those pivotal life moments where everything came together of its own accord, caught you by surprise and woke you up to the magic process of what it means to live life true to you.
Allow for it.

Hello, queen

I've been through so many rebirths within myself since I left my marriage. Every time I've reached a major point in myself, a place of deeper happiness, expression, creativity or love, I've thought, *Yes, I'm here.*

Only to discover that actually, no, I was not.

And so I begin being even more. I go deeper. I become even happier. I find more peace. I grow into and express even more of me.

To tell you this journey has been easy for me would be a lie. So many times I've wished for the easier path straight into some else's arms. And in some ways, I did have that path, until their arms weren't big enough to hold me, so I had to move on.

Growth, for me, has been amazing. It has been necessary. But it hasn't always been easy. It has been lonely. Deeply lonely at times. I share this because I know it's true at times for every woman who finds herself on this path.

The queen journey … there is no stop. No end point where we can declare, 'Oh, I'm here now.'

Before my grandfather passed away, he shared with me that he didn't really 'hit his straps' within himself until he reached his fifties. Everything was just a warm-up until then.

The more birthdays I have, the more I feel this.

This next season is only just starting for me, and I want to suggest to you that yours is too. Whether you're one month since leaving your marriage or ten years, you can begin hitting your straps now better than you ever have at any other time in your life.

You can start at any time too. So it might as well be now.

As my man crush, Matthew McConaughey, says, 'I don't want to just revolve. I want to evolve.' I feel that.

Life is short but we like to live it as though it's long, amassing things to take us through to the end, insisting and hoping that they must stay this way with us like a scrooge.

Why?

Whoever said that something you chose for yourself in your twenties or thirties (forties or fifties even), must stay this exact way for the rest of your life, otherwise it wasn't a success, in life, love, your career, your finances, or whatever it might be for you, was playing a cruel trick on you.

A very cruel one.

Success is reaching the end of your life and seeing how much you evolved and how all those dots joined together in magical, beautiful ways to lead you to where you are today.

It's ending your life in the place you desired to be, having lived feeling the way you desired to feel.

Your ninety-year-old self, sitting back in her rocking chair and looking over the entire depth and breadth of your life, can see this better than you right now. She can see your full life experience while you cannot. How every moment beautifully joined and led you to the next, aligned one.

Just keep being you, living your life true to you, is what I think she'd say if she were looking down on you in this moment.

Stop your doubting. Let others be who they are, and you start to embrace who you really are. Save your own self in the area you need saving, because you are capable, because no one else can but you can. Love again. Let yourself create something new and wonderful, something so outside of your own box that yourself in the past would be blown away to witness future you.

Just let yourself be where you are at, knowing this isn't always going to be where you are at.

Who knows where you are going to end up? Where life and your path will take you.

It could be absolutely anywhere.

What an exciting goddam thought.

With love to you,

Carla x

Acknowledgements

To all the individuals I have had the opportunity to coach and support personally through their divorce or relationship ending. I want to say thank you for being the inspiration and foundation behind *Seconds Please*.

Your path, combined with my own personal path, has allowed me the insight to put pen to paper and be able to create this work.

Thank you also to those individuals who have supported me professionally to move myself into this place of ease and grace within myself and within my life. Every piece of the puzzle that you helped me find and put words on has brought me to this moment today. I am forever grateful for your presence and your beautiful wisdom in my life.

About the Author

CARLA DA COSTA is a divorce coach and author of *Finding Love After Divorce: How to know if they're the one or just another one.* Carla has become a modern voice on marriage separation for women and men, and asks readers, is divorce truly a failure or could this be the best catalyst for change that has ever happened to you?

Through her private coaching practice, online programs and books, Carla works with people who are separated, divorced or divorcing, guiding them through these transformative experiences. Carla's practice supports and inspires women and men to make this next season of their life the best season of their life.

carladacosta.com
Facebook.com/carladacostaperth
Instagram: @carla_dacosta

CPSIA information can be obtained
at www.ICGtesting.com
Printed in the USA
LVHW102100260723
753569LV00007B/78

9 780645 139297